WITHDRAWN

Nothing Stands Still

NOTHING STANDS STILL / *Essays by Arthur M. Schlesinger*

Introduction by Arthur M. Schlesinger, Jr.

The Belknap Press of Harvard University Press

Cambridge, Massachusetts, 1969

Distributed in Great Britain by Oxford University Press, London
Library of Congress Catalog Card Number 69-18045
Printed in the United States of America

Contents

Introduction by Arthur M. Schlesinger, Jr.   1

I. THE SCHOLAR

  1. History   19
  2. Edward Eggleston: Evolution of a Historian   47
  3. An American Historian Looks at Science and
     Technology   65
  4. Political Mobs and the American Revolution,
     1765–1776   76
  5. The Lost Meaning of "The Pursuit of Hap-
     piness"   94
  6. Was Olmsted an Unbiased Critic of the
     South?   98

II. THE CITIZEN

  7. The New Tyranny   127
  8. The True American Way of Life   147
  9. War and Peace in American History   157
 10. Do We Have National Unity?   169
 11. Extremism in American Politics   180

Index   197

Nothing Stands Still

Introduction by

Arthur M. Schlesinger, Jr.

Arthur M. Schlesinger published two collections of essays in his lifetime—*New Viewpoints in American History* in 1922 and *Paths to the Present* in 1949 (with a revised and enlarged edition in 1963). The present volume brings together eleven essays not published in these previous collections. For sake of convenience, the book is divided into two parts: "The Scholar" includes the essays dealing with historical questions and "The Citizen" those dealing with public affairs. The reader will note, however, that to a degree the division is artificial. The essays written primarily for scholars in a number of cases take up problems of urgent concern to the citizen; and the essays on public issues, though addressed to non-professional audiences, are informed by a historian's understanding of social and political dilemmas.

The first three essays set forth some of my father's views on the direction in which professional history should evolve in the United States. In "History," meditating on the state of the art as it was forty years ago in terms which still seem all too relevant today, he argues for a conception of the discipline which would comprehend "the totality of man's experiences in the past." Along the way he offers useful observations about the role in the writing of history of historical laws, of documents and statistics, of the social and psychological sciences, of monography, and of self-deception. In "Edward Eggleston: Evolution of A Historian" he resurrects the career of a neglected pioneer of social history. The remaining essays in this section display historical dimensions of problems still very much with us. "An American Historian Looks at Science and Technology" touches on the question of what later became known as "the two cultures"; "Political Mobs and the American Revolution" illuminates the traditions of mass violence in the American democracy; "The Lost Meaning of 'The Pursuit of Happiness'" suggests some complexities in what was briefly known in 1968 as "the politics of happiness"; and "Was Olmsted an Unbiased Critic of the South?" considers the tragedy of black-white relations at an earlier stage in our history.

I do not suppose that it would have occurred to my father to reprint the first essay in the second section—"The New Tyranny," a commencement address he delivered at Ohio State University in 1926. I do so partly because the crispness and vigor of the presentation suggest some of the qualities which made him effective as a teacher, partly because it may interest another generation to show how many issues they consider peculiar to their own time—the mechanization of American culture, the militarization of American life, the organization man, the academic revolution—were identified and discussed forty years ago. This quotation may suggest the contemporary flavor of this remarkable address:

> The modern tyranny . . . is [not] so much an oppression of the body as it is of the inner life of man . . . It is the monstrous product of three factors in American development that in themselves should have yielded only good: Public Opinion, the Machine, and the National Genius for Organization. Grown to bloated dimensions, they have collectively imposed on the mind of man a servitude that is all the more fearful because it is impalpable and unseen, all the more powerful because it is seldom challenged.

And how familiar this passage will sound to those who have followed the turmoil on American campuses in the late nineteen sixties!

> The fact is that the whole system of higher education has been organized for the convenience and benefit of the teacher or specialist in a subject rather than from the point of view of the needs of the individual student . . . Leaders of opinion, reflecting the current subservience to industrial ideals, have been heard to speak approvingly of "educational factories" and of "mass production in education." The fact is, however, that the process of educating the human mind is not comparable to that of assembling and uniting the parts of an automobile . . . The situation will continue until the course

of study is completely reorganized with the learner's mind, rather than the teacher's, as the starting point of the educational process . . . Perhaps most significant of all has been the self-assertion of the students themselves in matters relating to educational policy. They are asking, and asserting, the right to be heard on questions which, though we have often ·forgotten it, are more vitally related to their interests than to those of the faculty.

"The New Tyranny" also bears an interesting relationship to the piece immediately following on "The True American Way of Life"—a piece written more than a quarter century later for a great American newspaper at the depth of the McCarthyite squalor of the early nineteen fifties. The next two essays show how historical understanding in the troubled twelve months after Pearl Harbor could throw light on public issues—on the tension between isolationism and internationalism in American history and on the problem of national unity in wartime (two themes he later elaborated in *Paths to the Present*). "Extremism in American Politics," his last article, was published a few weeks after his death in the autumn of 1965. It expressed his sense of the perennial conflict between fanaticism and rationality in the ordering of American affairs.

In an oral history interview, Dr. Saul Benison once asked my father about his "philosophy of history." "I confess," my father replied, "that that is a word that always intimidates me. There have been so many follies committed in terms of so-called philosophies of history that I would prefer . . . to put before you certain commonsense judgments about history which have grown out of my thinking about it and my practice of it." He observed in his autobiography *In Retrospect: The History of a Historian* (1963), "I am probably typical [of American historians] in thinking that a scholar renders his principal service in exemplifying the principles instead of discoursing on them."

From this interview and from other sources, one can reconstruct salient elements in my father's attitude toward history. Though he never saw history as an arcane study divorced from daily life or irrelevant to lay concerns, he had a strong sense of its distinctive value and discipline and therefore rejected the instrumental view of history current among some New Historians of the nineteen twenties. In his papers I found this scribbled note: "In my judgment the historian should not study the past with a determination to find ideas and events which are peculiarly significant for the present. This tends to distort the actual historical process and misrepresent the attitudes and beliefs of the time." History was thus to be studied for its own sake; the historian's fulfillment, at once aesthetic and technical, lay in acknowledging the autonomy of the past and striving to perceive the motives and patterns of another time without regard to contemporary preoccupations.

The essential thing about history, as he put it in another note, is that *"nothing stands still"* and the "moral" he drew from this was the need for "a liberal, flexible attitude." He knew, of course, that no historian could escape the blinkers of his own age and of his own psyche; "in an absolute sense . . . [objectivity] is an unattainable ideal."

Historical "facts" seemed to him subjective in a double
sense—first in the minds of the actors, then in the minds of
the investigators. All historical writing involved "incessant
selection" on the basis of the investigators' criteria; "it is
these assumptions that historians need to drag into the
open." Self-criticism could save historians from "self-
deception" and make them conscious of their own presuppositions. But "the difficulty of being objective is no
reason at all for ditching the ideal . . . To me, at least, it is
the hope that the finding of new relationships is leading
onward to a true picture, a true understanding, of this event
or activity in history." Without this "spiritual drive," the
historian "is falling short of the high calling which I believe
to be his." Therefore "self-appraisal is of the nature of
historical discipline . . . You notice all along I have never
used the term scientific . . . The historian must put himself
under the skin of the other person, see the world through
the eyes of these other people."

He added to Dr. Benison (though he crossed this sentence
out in going over the transcript) that he did not regard "fire
or excitement" as the essence of historical work. "A
Macaulay, by being a partisan, can excite you, but the mere
fact that he's become emotional is an added barrier to his
quest for truth . . . Any historian who makes simple moral
judgments is apt to be widely read. It's a very easy trick to
play, because the moral judgments of today differ from the
moral judgments of a hundred years ago. They are often
better, but not always." As he saw it,

> each generation should be judged by its own concepts of
> justice and ethics, not by later standards . . . Indeed, this

6

obligation to appraise human behavior according to the standards of the times seems to me to be the essence of what we call historical mindedness. It is, moreover, the only way of understanding how equally earnest and high-minded men could differ on such questions, say, as American independence, human slavery, the government control of industry. If you break down mankind into villains and virtuous people, it certainly is a terrific distortion . . . I would say it was dangerous for a modern historian to apply his own moral standards of his own time to what people had done in a previous generation, because that would imply to me something I don't believe in, that there is such a thing as absolute moral standards.

He also held back from the romantic tendency he noted in historians like Macaulay to dramatize the role of the individual in history. He tended to place his own emphasis on the role of ideas—"impersonal forces"—like religion, nationalism, democracy.

As I believe, the role of the individual, of the so-called "great man," has only been to speed or crystallize these deeper tendencies. Sam Adams was not essential for the success of the American revolutionary movement, nor was Jefferson or Jackson essential for the establishment of a broader democracy. My belief is that, if particular individuals had not come to the surface, others would have, and that because of our constant human tendency of simplification it's simpler to discuss human develop-

7

ment in terms of personality than it is in the duller
categories of social and economic and intellectual
movements.

My father's recoil from facile moralism and romanticism
helped shape his own conception of the historical enterprise.
His abiding determination was to do justice to the part that
"men in the mass" play in history and to portray the common
behavior and experience. He explained his idea of social
history in a note found in his papers (perhaps intended as
part of the preface for his last book, *The Birth of the Nation*):

> It assumes, what common observation confirms even of
> our own generation, that politics has seldom or for long
> been the major concern of society. Other goals—bread-
> winning, mating, personal immortality, self-improve-
> ment, personal power, the betterment of the community,
> the love of beauty—these and like interests have day in
> and out absorbed man's energies and thought. An
> understanding of the molding forces should go far to
> answer the question: why we behave like Americans.

His advocacy of social history sprang in part from his sense
as a youth of the irrelevance of conventional history to the
experience of the son of a German father and an Austrian
mother growing up in a small town in Ohio. History, as the
academic subject encountered in school and college, was
strictly Anglo-Saxon; its domain was politics, diplomacy, and
war. All this, as he later wrote, seemed "snobbish and
exclusive." Xenia, Ohio, was filled with Germans, Irish,
and Negroes; why then did the schoolbooks portray England

as the one and only mother country? (He raised this with his father who wryly commented that "apparently the only Germans worth mentioning were the Hessians who had fought on the wrong side in the War for Independence.") And why leave to journalists and novelists the fascinating story of the way plain people lived—worked, played, ventured, suffered—in the past?

These questions were on his mind even before he went to college. "Though my thoughts were immature and unformulated," he later wrote, "I could not help feeling there was something wanting in a history that skipped so much that seemed to me so important." A favorite quotation from Mr. Dooley summed it up:

> I know histhry isn't thrue, Hinnessy, because it ain't like what I see ivry day in Halsted Sthreet. If any wan comes along with a histhry iv Greece or Rome that'll show me th' people fightin', gettin' dhrunk, makin' love, gettin' married, owin' the grocery man an' bein' without hard-coal, I'll believe they was a Greece or Rome, but not befure . . . Th' other kind iv histhry is a post-mortem examination. It tells ye what a counthry died iv. But I'd like to know what it lived iv.

The boy in Xenia was not, of course, alone in questioning the conventional history of the day. When my father was twelve years old, Edward Eggleston in a presidential address to the American Historical Association on "The New History" argued for a shift from "drum and trumpet history" to a "history of culture, the real history of men and women."

NOTHING STANDS STILL

When my father went to Columbia University in 1910 for graduate study, he found a stimulating group of teachers— James Harvey Robinson, James T. Shotwell, and, above all, Charles A. Beard—insisting on the role of social, economic, and intellectual forces in history. This ferment within the profession was reinforced by the social and political pressures of the time. The quickening pace of immigration and urbanization, and the concurrent rise of sociology, were forcing new factors into the historian's equations, while in politics the Progressive movement was proclaiming the significance of mass needs and aspirations.

It was still not easy to shake university curricula from the familiar political, military, and diplomatic moorings. Returning in 1912 to teach at Ohio State, where he had taken his bachelor's degree two years before, my father had to wait seven years before he was permitted to lecture (and then only in summer school) on less orthodox aspects of American history. In the fall of 1919, he went to the University of Iowa as head of the history department and immediately introduced a course entitled "New Viewpoints in American History." In 1922 he made "New Viewpoints" into a book and initiated a new course on the "Social and Cultural History of the United States"—the first such course to be given in any college or university. When he went on to Harvard in 1924, this became the famous History 55, later History 163.

The effort to deal with "the totality of man's experiences in the past" compelled the early social historian to turn to specialized writings—histories of religion, education, science, journalism, the fine arts, and so on. These works, generally by practitioners in the particular fields, often discussed their subjects in a vacuum, as though the developments bore little relation to the general conditions of American society. If social history were to achieve academic maturity, my father came to feel, there had to be a cooperative effort by professional historians to portray "the formation and growth of civilization in the United States"—an effort in which the diverse actions and passions of men and women would be conceived "not separately and independently of one another but as an integral and integrated part" of American life. This was the genesis of the *History of American Life* series which he co-edited with Dixon Ryan Fox. As he later wrote, "Fox and I in planning this work aimed to free American history from its traditional servitude to party struggles, war and diplomacy and so show that it properly included all the varied interests of the people."

Looking back in 1957, my father noted several main points in the battle for social history. He had been first of all trying to raise social history "from the status of sheer antiquarianism and impressionistic description to the status of a genuine historical discipline." Next, he had wanted to bring certain forces, hitherto neglected, into the mainstream of American history. Thus he placed special emphasis—as in his own contribution to the *History of American Life* series, *The Rise of the City, 1878–1898* (1933)—on the city as a major factor in American development. He also wanted to give women, half the population, their rightful place in the growth of American civilization—a concern felicitously commemorated by the establishment at Radcliffe College of the Arthur and Elizabeth Schlesinger Library on the

NOTHING STANDS STILL

History of Women in America. And he had sought full recognition of the role of ethnic minorities in American life—not as a problem but as a process. For many years he was a member of the Board of Editors of the *Journal of Negro History*; in the nineteen thirties he laid aside his own work to put into final shape the posthumous writings of his friend Marcus Lee Hansen, the pioneer historian of American immigration (*The Atlantic Migration, 1607–1860* won the Pulitzer Prize in 1941); and toward the end of his life he laid aside his work again to serve as a member of the Fund for the Republic's Commission on the Rights, Liberties and Responsibilities of the American Indian. Beyond this, he always tried to see American history as a phase of world history and was an early champion of what is now known as "comparative history."

The triumph of this richer conception of history has been so complete in recent years that it is hard to remember what the argument was all about. A younger generation of historians, many of them my father's students, explored the issues and developed the themes of *New Viewpoints* and the *History of American Life*. Intellectual history, urban history, the history of immigration, the history of science—all are now routine in academic curricula. Even political and diplomatic history are increasingly presented as an expression of social, economic, and intellectual forces. Younger historians today employ without a second thought the methods and insights of the social sciences.

My father remained alert to gaps in the coverage of social history. In 1957 he enumerated the following areas as demanding further study: the role of the family in American

society ("the whole process of colonization was the movement of families"); the history of education; the role of voluntary associations; the evolution of American law; the history
of American science. In a 1960 talk before the Henry Adams
Club at Harvard he added as fields where promising work
was at last being done but which still needed further exploration: urban history, the role of women, and newspaper
history.

And he always hoped that more attention would be paid
to the problem of cycles in history. His celebrated essay
"The Tides of National Politics," published first in the *Yale
Review* in 1939 and then revised for *Paths to the Present*,
plotted the alternation between progressive and conservative—activist and passive—moods in American national
affairs.* This theory attracted the attention of political
leaders—among them Franklin D. Roosevelt and John F.
Kennedy—rather more than it did that of historians. In *In
Retrospect* my father wondered why the cyclical approach,
which economists had fruitfully applied to business fluctua-
tions,

> has not set historians to probing analogous recurrences
> in other fields of thought and action. Thus, in religion
> there have been persisting alternations of orthodoxy and

---

* He had been interested in this question since writing "Radicalism and
Conservatism in American History" for *New Viewpoints*. In 1924 he set
forth the cyclical theory in a talk at Nantucket. His forecast of a conservative
period till around 1932 produced from one of the audience an anguished
cry of "My God!" Afterward the expostulator introduced himself as David
K. Niles, then running the LaFollette-Wheeler campaign in Massachusetts
and later a special assistant to Presidents Roosevelt and Truman. The 1924
forecast contemplated a liberal period till about 1948 or 1950 and a conservative period till about 1960 or 1962.

heterodoxy, in literature of realism and romanticism, in the fine arts of classicism and experimentalism. Is it not worth inquiring whether these are simply haphazard phenomena, or, as may well be possible, expressions of an inherent and explicable rhythm?

As for social history in its general conception, he did not believe, as he wrote in 1963 in *In Retrospect*, that it had yet

issued beyond the stage of trial and error. Much of it is still of the taxonomic or descriptive variety, consisting of catalogues of facts grouped in appropriate categories and treated for their own sake instead of in relation to other developments of the times. Social history, maturely conceived, seeks to grasp and depict both the inner and outer life of society and to integrate the two, and for this there must be found a unifying theme inferred from a painstaking examination of the data.

The search for integration would involve the "recognition that disciplined insight is sometimes justifiable to bridge gaps in documented knowledge and that the suppression of personal bias is in the absolute sense unattainable."

As the monographic work in social and cultural history accumulated, my father came to feel that the time had come for a new synthesis. After his retirement from active teaching in 1954, he settled down in his study on Gray Gardens East to write a multi-volume history of the social and cultural development of the American people. Unfortunately, with his many commitments, public as well as scholarly, he lived only to complete the first volume—*The Birth of the Nation*, published in 1968 by his old friend Alfred A. Knopf.

Introduction by Arthur M. Schlesinger, Jr.

The division of this book between "The Scholar" and "The Citizen," as I suggested earlier, is somewhat artificial. My father saw the two functions as indivisible. While he was never a partisan in a way which threatened his professional detachment, he had a high sense of the responsibility of the scholar to democracy. "He was a patriot in the best sense," wrote his cherished colleague Samuel Eliot Morison, "a lover of his country, right or wrong, but always endeavoring to keep her faithful to the liberal tradition of the founding fathers."

He considered himself a political independent, but was a strong, though never uncritical, supporter of Wilson, Roosevelt, Stevenson, and Kennedy. No joiner by temperament, he did not hesitate to stand up and show himself when justice was at stake, from Sacco and Vanzetti and before to the American Indians and after. He took great pleasure in serving for a number of years as chairman of the Massachusetts United Labor Committee, in which the American Federation of Labor and the Congress of Industrial Organizations joined with Americans for Democratic Action in common political endeavor. He greatly enjoyed his work in the nineteen forties on the Commission on Freedom of the Press and his close association for many years with the Nieman Fellows at Harvard. He was active in the fight against Senator Joseph McCarthy.

Such secular intervention did not appear to him in conflict with the scholarly vocation; rather he considered civic commitment indispensable to the health of a society if free inquiry were to be possible. Emerson always seemed to him one of the wisest of Americans, and he responded throughout his life to the challenge of "The American Scholar."

NOTHING STANDS STILL

"There goes in the world," Emerson said,

> a notion that the scholar should be a recluse, a valetudi-
> narian—as unfit for any handiwork or public labor as a
> penknife for an axe . . . As far as this is true of the studi-
> ous classes, it is not just or wise. Action is with the
> scholar subordinate, but it is essential. Without it he is
> not yet man . . . I do not see how any man can afford, for
> the sake of his nerves and his nap, to spare any action
> in which he can partake . . . The true scholar grudges
> every opportunity of action past by, as loss of power.

The study of history, my father wrote in his memoir, "only
reinforced the belief that life, liberty, and the pursuit of
happiness constitute the birthright of every man and woman
and that a government of the people must strive tirelessly
to ensure its preservation."

His whole life was an act of faith in the reasonable and
temperate qualities of man. This faith was always realistic:
the belief in reason never overlooked the impulses toward
violence buried deep in human nature and in the American
past, nor was the moderation ever that of the man who cautiously seeks the middle of the road. Like the founders of
the republic, he had a robust vision of a community of liberty which honorable men must defend against those who
seek to replace freedom by fanaticism. He liked to quote
Jefferson: "I am one of those who think well of the human
character. I steer my bark with Hope in the head, leaving
Fear astern. My hopes indeed sometimes fail; but not oftener
than the forebodings of the gloomy."

As a scholar, he helped bring the common life of the people, their habits, beliefs, anxieties, and dreams, into the center of the historical enterprise. As a citizen, he incarnated a tempered and steadfast liberalism, skeptical of pretensions and dogmas, soberly, indestructibly optimistic about the future of the country he loved.

I THE SCHOLAR

1 History

History is at once one of the oldest and youngest branches of knowledge. The eager searcher for origins can trace it to the earliest days of man on earth. Whenever *Homo sapiens* recalled his past actions or made decisions in the light of former experiences, history was beginning to play a part in human affairs. Such history was of a very simple type, of course, not yet written, or organized into a body of learning, or subjected to critical analysis. At first hardly more than an individual's personal memory, in the course of time it began to take on the more imposing guise of tribal mythology or folklore. From such beginnings history has slowly and painfully developed through the travail of the centuries into the form it now possesses of a closely welded, severely critical discipline, with a technique and standards of its own, and cultivated mainly by specialists.

The long history of history attests its hoary antiquity; it is only when we realize that the human story always remains unfinished, teasing our interest with the familiar tag of "To be continued in our next," that we see why this ancient subject is perennially renewing its youth. The past is always dogging our heels, striving ceaselessly to banish the present,

Reprinted from Wilson Gee, ed., *Research in the Social Sciences: Its Fundamental Methods and Objectives* (New York: The Macmillan Company, 1929), 209–237.

and succeeding at least in reducing it to a thin disappearing line between the past and the future. The historian's materials are thus constantly accumulating as the present flees before the past and the span of the human story lengthens.

Whatever may be said of women in these modern days, the historian's work is never done. Indeed, his work is in constant danger of being undone, for new records often yield fresh information in regard to familiar events and suggest novel and unexpected interpretations. Like old Father William in the nursery jingle, history may at any time kick up its heels and do the unexpected. Lord Acton, lecturing on "The Study of History" at Cambridge in 1895, named the American Revolution as a subject whose main aspects were so thoroughly understood that the work on it need never be done over again. Yet in the years since this pronouncement more progress has been made in arriving at the truth of that episode than in all the years before, with results so shocking to the sensibilities of the voters of a great Middle Western city as to produce almost an international crisis. The new findings, it is interesting to note, were based in very small part on the unearthing of fresh evidence, but were derived chiefly from a reexamination of what was old and familiar.

In other cases, however, it has been the discovery of new materials which has given freshness and piquancy to this oldest of the social studies. Excavations in widely scattered parts of the world—in Egypt, Greece, Asia Minor, Tibet, Peru, Yucatan, Ohio—have produced a wealth of inscriptions, monuments, implements, and other remains which have enabled scholars to reconstruct the civilizations of early peoples and push back the existing limits of knowledge. Modern history has benefited perhaps as greatly through gaining access to sources hitherto withheld from scholarly use. In recent years whole libraries and collections of manuscripts have for the first time been made available to students. The Vatican Library was thus opened by Leo XIII, and as a result of the World War the government archives of Russia, Austria, and Germany may be examined by all comers. All together, countless thousands of new documents have been added to those possessed by historians a generation or so ago.

Much has been written in regard to the uses to which history has been put in different ages. Until comparatively recent times history was looked upon as a legitimate branch of propaganda—for church or for state, for the *status quo* or for radical social change—and, as contemporary events have shown, this attitude still can count on a certain amount of public favor. It has been cultivated almost as generally as a form of didactic or imaginative literature. Not until our own time has history declined the role of conscript and become a soldier in its own right. But even under these auspicious circumstances, with the student seeking objective truth as his only goal, the preconceptions of the age, as well as his own human shortcomings, almost certainly refract the historian's vision and affect the results of his researches.

These ulterior influences are stubborn facts which, as we shall see, the historian accepts as a part of the difficulties of his task, and, accepting them frankly, may in some measure counteract. In these respects, however, history does not stand alone among the social studies. The dogmatist in any one of these fields would do well to reflect that each age has formulated its own economics, its own conception of ethics, its own political theory, and that, so far as we are warranted in judging, scholarly work along these lines will always be conditioned by the "climate" peculiar to the period in which the student does his work. Even such exacting nonsocial disciplines as chemistry and astronomy trace their lineage respectively to alchemy and astrology, and in the present generation continue to change rapidly under the hands of the workers.

I

The main concern of the present discussion is not with history in other ages and climes, but with history in our own time and primarily in America. Indeed, one does not have to leave the borders of the United States in order to observe how the content and outlook of historical writing have been influenced by changing ideals of scholarship and the shifting interests of society. In the first decades of national independence the writers of history believed it unpatriotic to allow the public to see great national heroes in their unguarded moments—*en dishabille,* as one of them put it. When Jared Sparks, professional historian and president of Harvard, undertook to edit the writings of Washington, he altered and "embellished" the language so as to set the Father of His Country firmly on his pedestal. It may also be noted, in passing, that he omitted Washington's uncomplimentary references to the people of New England. At a humbler social and scholarly level was his contemporary, "Parson" Weems, who, as everyone knows, invented the cherry-tree legend and gave posterity the conception of an impossible Washington which still lives in the minds of most people despite all efforts of later writers to combat it.

The age of historical mythology gave way to the democratic upheaval of Jackson's times and a lyric belief in the divinely appointed mission of the plain people. It was during these years that George Bancroft began his gargantuan labors, collecting and consulting great masses of hitherto unused documents and, by his thoroughness, laying the foundations of modern historical scholarship. An ardent democrat and a leader of Jackson's party, Bancroft scanned the horizon of early America for evidences of the irrepressible conflict between democracy and despotism, and reported his results in the incandescent rhetoric of a Fourth-of-July orator. As the passion for popular rights was merged in the bitterness of sectional controversy, another shift occurred in the historians' point of view, and the two decades after Appomattox saw them engaged in conducting a postmortem on the past from the standpoint of the outcome of the Civil War. Along with these main currents of historiography went minor eddies and side currents. Reflecting a European fashion, Prescott, Motley, and Parkman demonstrated that history might also be literature. They were assiduous in research, but their principal purpose was to treat the past as a pageantry of stirring incidents and dramatic personalities. The writings of this group, however, were little concerned with the central themes of American development.

The present school of history in America, the so-called scientific school, dates from the eighties of the last century. Its rise synchronized with the expansion of the natural sciences and the growth of the scientific spirit in all fields of human inquiry. As in the case of the other social studies, many of its leaders were trained in German universities.

Returning to America, they established historical seminars at Johns Hopkins, Harvard, Columbia, and other strategic centers, from which went forth an increasing stream of young scholars to fertilize remoter academic communities and train up disciples of their own. The advent of the modern school marked a sharp break with the historiography of the earlier period. The sole concern of the new historians was to reconstruct a true record of the life of mankind without fear or favor. They strove to scrutinize the past in the same dispassionate way that a surgeon does a patient upon whom he is about to operate and to state their findings accurately and truthfully. With them the propagandist or the literary uses of history were entirely supplanted by the ideal of scientific detachment.

The fruits of their labors are embodied in an impressive mass of writings which form the firm basis of our knowledge of American history today. Methodologically, the system of research they inaugurated was a democratic one since it involved a microscopic examination of myriad data and required antlike activity on the part of countless numbers of workers. The great exemplars of American historiography of earlier times—the writers of full-length histories—rapidly yielded ground to the masters of the monograph—to those who knew some fragment of history supremely well—for no longer could intuition or a vivid imagination be allowed to fill a gap which might be closed by intensive research. The comprehensive histories characteristic of the new age have taken the form of collaborative enterprises by specialists, or have been fashioned by skilled joiners who fitted together the bits of new truth scattered in a hundred articles and monographs, or have represented the joint efforts of bands of hired researchers directed by captains who applied to historical scholarship the hustling methods of modern business.

Equally typical of the new era was the attention given to making available sources and records hitherto uncollected or unknown to the scholarly world. This was indeed a far-sighted program, to which governmental agencies, libraries, historical societies, and private individuals lent a helping hand. Rare documents were reprinted, or reproduced through the photostatic process; important collections of manuscripts were put into type for the first time. A guild of historical experts grew up whose standards of editorship were so carefully maintained that textual criticism has played a comparatively small part in American historical research. Their services were supplemented by the compilation of innumerable bibliographies, indexes, calendars, archival guides, and bibliographies of bibliographies, all designed to suggest to the seeker other possible sources of information.

The founders of the modern school devoted themselves mainly to political, constitutional, and military history. There was no inherent reason why this should be so, for their highly refined methodology might have been turned with profitable results to other phases of the human past. But they worked in accordance with the best European traditions, and by exploring carefully the evolving political framework of society, they disposed of a whole series of problems which have touched the interests of later historians at many points. It is no reproach to them to say that the studies they produced were primarily descriptive or systematic in character, little concerned with the hidden motivation of events. In this respect they were doing for the subsequent development of history what the pioneer workers in the natural sciences did for their successors.

II

As might be expected, the modern school of history has itself been subject to transforming influences similar to those which in other times caused the outlook of scholars to change from generation to generation. In his presidential address before the American Historical Association in 1900, Edward Eggleston was already demanding a "New History"; James Harvey Robinson reiterated the plea with much cogency and persuasiveness in a volume bearing that title in 1911; and more recently the same idea has been presented to the younger members of the profession with something like missionary zeal by Harry Elmer Barnes. These recurrent expressions of dissatisfaction have led to considerable misunderstanding outside the ranks of the historical guild. Not even the most active dissenters have expressed any wish to discard the basic ideals which animated the founders of the modern school, such as thoroughness of research, rigorous objectivity and accuracy in the statement of results. Their quarrel has been, rather, with the restricted range of interests of the older historians and, to some degree, with certain alleged shortcomings of their methodology. The dissenters have by no means won the field; the battle is being waged hotly on all fronts; but that they will meet with eventual success seems assured by the new social and intellectual circumstances in which society finds itself in the twentieth century.

26

Contemporary experience has emphasized as never before the importance of economic and technological factors in the life of man as compared with the political. The growth of gigantic business enterprises, the vast accumulations of capital, the deeply intrenched labor movement, the increasing dependence of society on science and invention, the dominance of economic questions in domestic and international politics—facts like these have caused historians to revaluate the materialistic forces in the life of mankind. A few scholars have frankly become economic determinists; all have been inclined to move such human interests as food, shelter and clothing nearer to the foreground of attention. In the light of such considerations political rivalries and partisan intrigues seem but shadow-symbols of greater struggles going on somewhere behind the screen, significant chiefly as indicative of these mightier forces. The historian of the new school is still on a hunt for these underlying forces, for he believes that if he can find them he will have the key with which to explain the motivation of events at a given time. Political history may perchance furnish him with some useful clues, but it is only as a means, not as an end in itself, that it continues to engage his attention.

Of course, the historian is always in danger of reading into the past motives that were not actually present or active. Certain modes of conduct are peculiar to the growing complexity and artificiality of our civilization; others seem generally characteristic of men in their behavior as social beings. The historical student needs constantly to be on his guard: he must be willing to discard a clever or novel interpretation for one which conforms to the known circumstances of the period he is studying. Nevertheless the path to understanding lies in the direction of seeing the past with ever fresh vision. New insights often make it possible to strip the past of the rationalizations of motive and desire that may have paraded, for example, under such garbs as religion or dynastic glory or national patriotism.

The new appreciation of economic motivation in human conduct has been accompanied by a realization of the part that men in the mass play in history. If modern science and technology are based on the importance of common things, modern society may be said to rest on the importance of common people. The older history was essentially snobbish and exclusive, paying no attention either to the "Unknown Soldier" or the nameless civilian. The proponents of the newer view maintain that history must embrace all sections of the population, poor as well as rich, women as well as men, the masses as well as the classes. Indeed, so many of the significant movements of the past have had their origins in obscure places (and none of them presumably has operated in a vacuum) that the Great-Man theory of history shows signs of being deflated in favor of one which views the Great Man as merely the mechanism through which the Great Many have spoken.

The historian's point of view has been further affected by the rapidly shrinking dimensions of the world. This has led to a new appreciation of the essential unity of mankind. For a century or more scholars, writing with strong nationalistic prepossessions, have dwelt upon the differences between peoples, stressing constantly *national* policies, aptitudes, aspirations. The events of our own day are causing students to think more in terms of similarities and common traits. They are asking, To what extent do nations act alike? rather than, In what respects may they be regarded as peculiar to themselves? As a result, one of the engrossing interests of the historian is coming to be the international movement of ideas, manners, and institutions, whether in the field of industrialism, political behavior, or religion. In looking back over the past it is clear that nations have never been independent entities except in a very restricted sense. Even the "splendid isolation" of the United States, with its advantages of geographic aloofness, has been largely a myth. As Professor Haskins pointed out in his presidential address to the American Historical Association in 1922, "Ireland has a potato famine in 1848, and Boston has an Irish mayor in 1922. Karl Marx and Engels publish their Communist Manifesto in this same 1848, and two generations later Bolshevism appears in the lumber camps of the Pacific Northwest." The slavery problem has been exhaustively treated as an American problem; but its relation to the world-wide movement for abolition is as yet little understood, though it is clear that the United States lagged behind the progressive European countries and was even out-distanced by the "backward" republics of Latin America.

It remains to be added that the new growths in the vineyard of history have been due, in no small part, to cross fertilization from other fields of social investigation. In America economics, political science, sociology, and history became professionalized subjects about the same time; and though the urge to intense specialization tended to raise barriers between them, in the course of time there was a certain amount of interpenetration and exchange of experience. In this process history has been notably indebted to economics; less so to political science because of the early preference historians showed for political subject matter. The influence of sociology is perhaps best seen in the growing attention given to such matters as the historical aspects of immigration and to the part played by religion and social reform in American history. In the field of world history such subjects as anthropology, ethnology, and archaeology have greatly enriched our knowledge of life in the past. As the historian has become more interested in *Kulturgeschichte*, he has similarly derived much value from the historical work performed by specialists in branches like the fine arts, literature, education, and science.

This account suggests that much of the progress of history in content and point of view has been due to impulses and pressures from outside. That this is in some measure true cannot be denied, nor can it be gain-said that the new developments have often been frowned upon by leaders of the profession. The first important work in the field of American economic history was performed by men who counted themselves economists, not historians; the first important American critique of the economic interpretation of history was likewise the work of an economist. The modern point of view in regard to the American Revolution receives much of its authority from the researches and writings of a Philadelphia lawyer. When the time came to write a dispassionate history of the Civil War and Reconstruction, the task was undertaken, not by a trained historian but by a retired captain of industry. The first man to project and begin a comprehensive *Kulturgeschichte* of America was an ex-Methodist clergyman, and the man who has piled volume upon volume of a *History of the People of the United States* first won his spurs as a teacher of civil engineering. There may be a moral here for those historians who at the present time view with indifference or hostility the impingement of new ideas on their sacred precincts.

III

History, strictly speaking, has no content of its own: it is a method of inquiry. History is always the history of something, not a study apart. The founders of the modern school, as we have seen, applied the historical method to government and politics. Gradually its scope has been broadened, so that today history is becoming concerned—in the hands of some, is already concerned—with the totality of man's experiences in the past. No aspect of these experiences can be safely neglected, for there is nothing man has thought or done or hoped or feared that has not left its mark in some manner on the life of society. Thus history is as many-sided as life itself. The historical point of view has far-reaching implications for scholarship in all fields. It enormously enlarges the range of observed phenomena, gives a sense of the relativity of present forms, and suggests the forces at work in contemporary society.

Nor would history disappear as a separate discipline if the scholars in the various fields of knowledge should work out their own specialized histories. A collection of the histories of art, law, religion, etc., would not constitute a history of mankind; the social process as a whole would still remain to be articulated and explained. History is one; and if scholars at times find it convenient to isolate certain threads for intensive study, it must not be forgotten that it is merely for the sake of convenience and that these several strands are tightly woven into a common pattern that is really indivisible. Like the historian, the sociologist is also interested in explaining the past, but he has not the historian's preoccupation with time-and-place relationships, being interested (as I understand it) chiefly in generalized descriptions of social behavior and in the evolution of successive types of society. The historian and the historical sociologist complement each other; their sympathetic cooperation is to be desired from the standpoint of the interests of both fields of study.

The acceptance of this broader conception of history will sooner or later necessitate far-reaching adjustments in regard to the equipment for research work. Editors and compilers of documents will have to expand their operations into the nonpolitical departments of social conduct, so as to include business papers, religious records, the minutes of reform bodies, and the like. The problem of selecting representative documents and anticipating the varied interests of investigators will under these circumstances be infinitely more difficult than ever before, and students will be compelled to do proportionately more work in manuscript collections. This, in turn, will impose on research libraries the burden of broadening their program of collecting source records so as to embrace the multifarious aspects of human life in the past. A beginning has been made with the organization of special historical collections dealing with business, transportation, religious denominations, agriculture, and similar interests; but these collections need development and many important domains of human enterprise remain untouched.

How can students be trained in our graduate schools to deal competently with the enormously expanded content of history? This basic problem has received little or no attention from those who occupy the seats of authority; for the most part, graduate instruction continues to be organized along the lines laid down a generation ago. Much hard, careful thinking will be necessary, and a considerable amount of experimentation, before a satisfactory solution can be reached. So far as the student of American history is concerned, he must, in addition to his present preparation, be familiar with all the great ideas and movements that have transformed the modern world and America as a part of it. All students, whether of American or other history, must be better rooted than at present in the methods and points of view of the related social fields, including psychology, and possess a good working knowledge of statistics. Besides they ought to be encouraged, if not required, to range widely in science, literature, and the arts. The historian of the future is evidently a creature not to be envied, and the doctoral examinations of the next generation may well be "weltering fields of the tombless dead."

IV

It is an ancient reproach, still echoed in many a luckless schoolroom, that history is only an exercise in the memorizing of dates. The taunt would be better founded today if historians were charged with being too factual-minded. All conquest of the unknown begins with the discovery of facts; and in the field of history this process is, in the very nature

33

of things, a continuing one. Yet history would be a barren subject indeed if it never advanced beyond the attainments of the catalogue and the dictionary. It cannot be denied, however, that many historians fail to show in their writings any growth beyond their graduate apprenticeship, and that even the works of seasoned scholars too often show traces of what might be called the "Ph. Disease." It was in reaction against this condition of affairs that the late Theodore Roosevelt—not then foreseeing that he would sometime become president of the American Historical Association—wrote to his friend Sir George M. Trevelyan:

> We have a preposterous little historical organization which, when I was just out of Harvard and very ignorant, I joined . . . After a while it dawned on me that all of the conscientious, industrious, painstaking little pedants, who would have been useful people in a rather small way if they had understood their own limitations, had become because of their conceit distinctly noxious. They solemnly believed that if there were only enough of them, and that if they only collected enough facts of all kinds and sorts, there would cease to be any need hereafter of great writers, great thinkers.

There can be no doubt that a widening chasm has been created between the professional historian and the reading public because of the devotion of the former to the unending task of gathering what Roosevelt called "bricks and stones." An eager public acclaim greeted the volumes of Bancroft, Motley, and Parkman as they issued from the press, whereas an epochal historical work passes unnoticed today unless mayhap it be crowned by some prize award. The public still reads history, but prefers easy nourishment in the form of syntheses and "outlines" prepared by persons who, as someone has said, write "without fear and without research." The historian's difficulty is partly one of literary style, but is perhaps even more largely the result of what might be called an occupational complaint.

Even within professional ranks many signs indicate a growing conviction that specialization to be fruitful must be fertilized by generalization. Perhaps the most striking evidence of this belief has been the revival of interest in the subject of historical laws. Some scholars blandly dismiss this interest as a twentieth-century reincarnation of the early-nineteenth-century preoccupation with the philosophy of history—a recrudescence of ancient superstition, as it were. If this is true, the fact would appear to illustrate a tendency of historical phenomena to repeat themselves, which these very critics, under other circumstances, would be the first to deny. It is only fair to say that the analogy is more apparent than real; for the present-day speculation rests upon a vast accumulation of objective data not before available; it does not aspire to answer the riddle of the universe; and it is being carried on, not as was the study of the philosophy of history by poets, philosophers, and theologians, but by historians of established reputation.

In his presidential address of 1908 before the American Historical Association Professor George Burton Adams declared his conviction that "the events with which it [history] is concerned have been determined by forces which act according to fixed law, and that most of the objections which have been urged against this view are due to misapprehensions, or incomplete reflection." A later president,

THE SCHOLAR

Professor Edward P. Cheyney, in 1923 courageously supported his adherence to the same doctrine by a tentative
formulation of six historical laws. "I do not conceive of these
generalizations," he stated,

> as principles which it would be well for us to accept,
> or as ideals which we may hope to attain; but as natural
> laws, which we must accept whether we want to or
> not; whose workings we cannot obviate, however much
> we may thwart them to our own failure and disadvan-
> tage; laws to be reckoned with, much as are the laws
> of gravitation, or of chemical affinity.

Credentials quite as respectable and much more numerous
might be offered in support of the opposite position. The
controversy turns, in first instance, on the question of what
is the proper province of the historian; whether history
should concern itself only with unique and hence unre-
peatable phenomena, or whether it may not also be concerned with studying the underlying forces and influences
that condition social growth and which, by their very nature,
seem to be constantly operative. The one point of view,
pushed to its extreme, would give an episodical account of
man's development, a mere sightseer's report of the surface
of the past. The other, if carried to its logical limits, would
yield a speculative, theorized interpretation so meagerly
stocked with evidence as to render dubious its claim to the
name of history at all. But neither group would accept such
statements as fairly representing their aims; nor can they
be said to do so.

As a matter of fact, the two points of view are not mutually
exclusive. It would seem folly to deny that there are two

36

aspects of the history of man. One consists of the exceptional or extranormal happenings; the other of the common or persistent factors. There is room for the study of both: the desirability of preserving the historical uniqueness of events or personalities need not preclude the quest for fundamental continuing forces and conditions, for irresistible tendencies and cyclical variations. A father of the Church once described the Holy Scripture as being at the same time a deep ocean in which the leviathan could wallow and a shallow pool in which an infant might play. Without suggesting which is monster and which babe, one is warranted in affirming that history is a large enough sea for both to bathe in.

If it be said that the assumption of the reign of law in history is unscientific, who can say that it is more scientific to assume that the development of man as a social being has been casual, fortuitous, uncontrolled by law? One hypothesis would appear to have as much scientific validity as the other. Plainly the jury requires further evidence before bringing in a verdict; and meanwhile a provisional sentence of "hard labor" imposed on both parties to the suit would greatly assist in advancing our knowledge as to the central issue involved.

For the immediate future, as the historian comes to occupy himself more and more with the life of the people and his interest is increasingly fixed on mass movements and emotions, the attention addressed to the discovery of historical laws is certain to grow greater. The difficulties that lie athwart the seeker's path might well deter the stoutest heart because of the profuseness and complexity of the data to be analyzed and the impossibility of establishing control conditions. Yet, as Professor Cheyney has suggested, the laws that govern the progress of human affairs should be no more difficult to fathom than, say, the laws that govern the winds and the tides; and no one doubts that these can be reduced to scientific statement.

It has been urged that if or when the historian discovers his laws, they will turn out to be sociological laws. "The voice is Jacob's voice, but the hands are the hands of Esau." Should this prediction come true, the result will, from a scientific point of view, be immensely reassuring. Social science will be merely repeating the experience of natural science, where workers in different fields (as recently in the exploration of the atom) often arrive at the same results and serve as a check on each other. Seekers for truth will hardly quarrel over the credit of discovery. Methodologically the law in question will deserve to be called "historical" in so far as it was revealed by the technique used by the historian; it will be equally entitled to be known as "sociological" to the extent that it was discovered by the procedures of the sociologist.

V

The question of whether history is a science has long been a favorite subject for disputation among dialecticians in the social fields. Yet the issue seems simple enough. If the term is confined to subjects where the phenomena operate in accordance with fixed law, history has not yet established its right to the label. If it attaches only to subjects in which the conclusions can be tested by experimental verification, obviously history is not so to be classed. But if the term may be applied to fields in which the methods of inquiry are critical and objective and the results win a consensus of acceptance by trained investigators, then history deserves the name as much as any branch of physical science.

The critical methodology which obtains in the field of history began in Germany with the work of Niebuhr and Ranke in political history, Baur and the Tübingen school in sacred history and F. A. Wolf in classical philology. It has been refined and elaborated by students since then and has formed the subject matter of scores of important treatises in divers languages. In general, the principles of evidence applied by the historian resemble those employed by a court of law. Did the witness tell the truth? Did he possess a conscious or unconscious bias? Was he capable of observing fully and accurately or judging correctly? Do his words properly express the thought he intended to convey? Did he write down his observations at the time or in later years? Yet the lawyer's task in cross-examining his witnesses is simple in comparison, for the historian in his work combines the functions of detective, prosecuting attorney, lawyer for the defendant, judge, and jury.

The results attained by this procedure have been so valuable that certain of its deficiencies usually pass unnoticed. One is the almost exclusive attention given to documented facts. When political history was the absorbing interest, this made little difference since major political decisions were usually found in the form of statutes, decrees, treaties, constitutions, and other formal pronouncements and were, moreover, likely to find mention in the personal papers of the time. But with history becoming socialized, reliance upon documentation often gives a misleading emphasis. So long as the stream of everyday life flows quietly along, it makes little mark on the annals of the time; it is only when it threatens to dry up or overflow its banks that its behavior is likely to attract contemporary notice. The sentiments felt most profoundly by a people, if in harmony with the existing social order, leave perhaps only incidental trace for the analyst, while the most casual exception may excite current attention and so assume exaggerated importance in the eyes of the later investigator.

There arises also the perennially baffling question as to whether the professions of a group as formally set forth correspond with their practice. Is Puritanism as a living religion in colonial New England better revealed by the Sabbath pulpit deliverances, of which we have ample record, or by the superstitious practices and irregular sex unions to which we know, from meager evidence, many of the lowly were addicted? The historical inquirer should not rely too piously on documentary testimony. Like the artist or the pioneering scientist, there are times when he must be willing to warm up his "cold facts" with his powers of insight and common sense and thus, by means of his constructive imagination, recapture the living past.

One other presupposition of historical methodology calls for a word of caution. The investigator is alert to the frailties and failings of the human beings whose records he examines, and these he discounts when constructing his narrative. But he usually assumes that the objectivity, to which he himself aspires as an ideal, is a quality which he possesses in fact. This is a dubious assumption when, as historians know, the foremost thinkers in all ages were fettered by their times, by their social sympathies, economic wants, or partisan bias, and when, as any psychologist knows, the finest intentions of conscious intelligence are likely to be ambushed by influences of which it may be wholly ignorant.

It is in the interest of scientific history to recognize frankly that historical "facts" are subjective in a double sense. In first instance they are entangled in the mental and emotional processes of the actors in the drama; at the next remove they are subject to the mental and emotional chemistry of the investigator's mind. Is objectivity, then, an impossible achievement? In an absolute sense, yes; for both the conception of a situation and the inferences of the historian are conditioned by his whole personality, which in turn is the product of his original endowment plus his life experience. But, relatively speaking, he may count on advancing the outposts of knowledge if he will subject his own mental processes to the same critical scrutiny that he does the source data with which he works.

Historians sometimes say that in undertaking a piece of research their minds are a perfect blank as to what they expect to find. An elementary knowledge of psychology shows that this attitude is one of self-deception. Even in the most matter-of-fact historical writing the process of inquiry is one of incessant selection, of determining which facts are important and which trivial; and the choices made rest upon certain criteria of importance and triviality which are implicit in the investigator's mind. It is these assumptions that historians need to drag into the open. In a work of historical scholarship the author might well devote his introduction to an exposition of his presuppositions; and in the learned journals the book reviewers might profitably direct a part of their fire at these same background considerations of the author.

VI

Statistics is a handmaid of history as it is of so many other branches of inquiry. The statistical method is a means of extracting the significant truths concealed in masses of numerical facts. Thus far historians have made only perfunctory use of diagrams and tabulations, but extraordinarily fruitful results have been attained by interpreting quantitative data in terms of maps. Analysis of the groupings of party votes in connection with the geographic distribution of cultural opportunities and of classes of property has yielded new insights, or confirmed surmises, as to the forces actually operating in politics. Professor Frederick J. Turner, perhaps our greatest master of this technique, was able, for instance, to reach the interesting, if disturbing, conclusion that

> The rough country, the least valuable farm lands, the illiterate counties tend, by and large, to be Democratic, as do the principal immigrant populations of the greater cities. The favored soil regions, the least illiterate areas, the most highly capitalized and industrial districts tend to be anti-Democratic, Federal, Whig, Republican, according to the area.

Detailed map analyses have enabled historians to penetrate behind the artificial barriers of political subdivisions and discover regionalisms that not only transcended state lines but divided states within themselves. The careful historian no longer speaks of the South but of the Souths, not of the West but of the Wests.

The possibilities of chartographic-statistical studies have as yet scarcely been plumbed. "History is an enterprise in space as well as in time," and as Professor Dixon Ryan Fox has recently pointed out, just as political history has benefited from map studies of successive physical frontiers, so social history offers an opportunity for plotting the succession of what might be called culture-frontiers. Where, at a particular time, was the public-education frontier, the bookstore frontier, the magazine-circulation frontier, the fraternal-organization frontier, the professionalized-sports frontier, the theater-supporting frontier? It is hardly necessary to say that much painstaking, fundamental research of this character will be necessary to give to social history the substance and validity that is rightly claimed for the work of the political historians.

The statistical method has its pitfalls, of course. The basic data often require critical evaluation. Thus, as is well known, the census of 1870 is very unreliable as a source of information in regard to Southern conditions. Moreover, quantitative measurements can properly be applied only to the outward signs, the external aspects, of social behavior, whereas complete understanding calls for inferences which are never based solely on numerical data. At most, statistics can only measure measurable things; and it would be highly imprudent for the historical scholar to assume that only those motives and forces are significant that can be recorded by an adding machine.

VII

Obviously a correct understanding of human nature is basic to the work of the historian. We have already seen that the student must apply psychological criteria in determining the value of his source evidence, and that it is desirable for him to bare his own mental and emotional prepossessions. A knowledge of psychology plays perhaps an even more important part when the historian comes to interpret the motives and actions of the men and women with whom his narrative is concerned. This is a thing apart from the dependability of his source materials. However well the surface appearance of an incident may be established or however plausible the contemporary explanations of the reasons for things, the inner meaning of events must, in final analysis, be explained in terms of the historian's own understanding of the motivation of human conduct.

Our age has a marked bias for mechanical explanations, and the tendency of the historian has been to reduce human nature to a formula. Historical interpretation is largely posited on the theory that mental processes are governed by reason, by intelligence, by conscious, deliberate, thought-out arguments. On the pages of the historian man is too often a mere logical machine actuated by self-interest. If modern psychology has done nothing else, it has disposed of this simple conception of human nature and has shown that the mental make-up of man is, like itself, a matter of infinite variety. Reason is important enough to set us apart from the lower animals; yet it is demonstrable that all but a very small fraction of our acts are attributable to instincts, urges, and drives that we share, in varying degree, with the brutes. Instead of a reasoning machine the human animal is seen to be a complex creature of impulse, habit, emotional preference, and autonomic reflexes, who occasionally directs his irrational desires to some intelligent end. Reason is but the arbiter among often unruly and conflicting impulses. Under the circumstances all that the historian can reasonably hope to accomplish is, first, to appreciate the intricate nature of man's mentality and, secondly, to seek to ascertain the motive or motives dominant in a particular situation.

The historians as a profession have as yet remained indifferent to the findings of the new psychology. Historical works continue to contain naïve speculations as to the springs of human action, or, if perchance the time-honored explanations are discarded, the writer is likely to fall into the opposite pit of attributing to others motives such as he recognizes in himself. It is, of course, true that in many instances adequate psychological data are lacking for a well-rounded interpretation of historical situations, but it is also true that from time immemorial historians have not hesitated to give what they might describe as a "common-sense" explanation of the same events. The real issue that is raised is whether, even in such doubtful instances, historians should not arm themselves with the new hypotheses and knowledges of human motivation which modern psychology has laid bare. If to do this it becomes necessary, as someone has suggested, to join a Psychology-of-the-Month Club, the benefits assured should prove amply worth the pains.

In concluding this memorandum on the objectives and methods of research in history, one is impressed with the thoughts that the workers in the field are of many minds, that they disagree in certain important respects, and that they represent differing and often conflicting tendencies. This situation, it may be observed, is regarded with the utmost complacence by the historians themselves. If the subject of history is in a state of transition, they cherish the comforting assurance that it has always been a transition, and there are some among them so unregenerate as to hope that such may ever be the case. Sufficient agreement in regard to the fundamentals of method exists as to permit the widest possible diversity of interest in the choice of individual projects of research. There is no possibility that the foundations laid so firmly by the modern critical school will ever be discarded. Growth and change will be in the direction of the improvement of present procedures and the conquest of new areas of truth.

2 Edward Eggleston: Evolution of a Historian

Edward Eggleston, well known to an earlier generation as author of the popular novel, *The Hoosier Schoolmaster*, appears here in his less familiar guise of a social and cultural historian. American historical writers have arrived at their calling in strange and divers ways. Today they are usually the products of graduate schools; but until the latter part of the nineteenth century, when professional training first became available, they were self-taught. Moreover, they nearly always cultivated history as an afterthought, since they felt the need to attain a firm financial footing before chancing the uncertain rewards of scholarship. Of Eggleston's contemporaries, for example, John Bach McMaster started out as a civil engineer, James Schouler made a prior reputation as a legal writer, George Bancroft devoted many years of his life to politics and the public service, and James Ford Rhodes was a retired industrialist. Francis Parkman and Henry Adams, both born to wealth, were the shining exceptions, though Adams served briefly and regretfully as a Harvard professor of history.

Fortunately, history is not a recondite subject girt with impregnable barriers; hence it was possible for men of

Reprinted from Edward Eggleston, *The Transit of Civilization: From England to America in the Seventeenth Century,* with a new introduction © 1959 by Arthur M. Schlesinger (Boston: Beacon Press, 1959), vi–xix.

studious bent, insight and critical acumen to make significant contributions, as all these men did. Moreover, unlike most of their successors of the so-called scientific school, they preferred the large canvas to the miniature, the rounded treatment to the monograph, and they strove to interest the general public rather than communicate only with fellow students.

Of this eminent company, Edward Eggleston was a worthy member. Turning to historical writing later in life than the others, he also brought to it an extraordinarily rich endowment. Born on December 10, 1837, at Vevay, a backwoods hamlet of the Indiana bank of the Ohio River, he was the son of Joseph Cary Eggleston, of colonial Virginia ancestry, who had migrated from the Old Dominion three years before to practice law in the rude settlement. Edward's mother, Mary Jane Craig, was the daughter of a nearby farmer and former Indian fighter, who had crossed the Alleghenies in 1781 and built the first blockhouse on the Indiana side of the stream. Little wonder that the Eggleston children found "the daring adventures of the generation before us" far more absorbing than the storybook account of Little Red Riding-hood and the wolf.

The youth obtained most of his education outside the classroom, probably no handicap in view of the bad teaching in country schools. He was a voracious reader, levying upon his father's library, which outnumbered any in the vicinity, and borrowing additional books whenever he could. He also spent long periods on the Craig farm, where he shared in tending the apple orchard as well as slaughtering pigs, rendering lard, and making soap. "In many households," he recalled in after years, "the old customs still held sway; the wool was carded, spun, dyed, woven, cut and made up in the house."

From infancy he imbibed a belief in a hidebound form of Methodism, which was heightened when his mother, four years after her husband's death in 1846, married a Methodist minister, William Terrell. This union caused the family to reside from time to time in various parts of Indiana—at New Albany and Madison as well as Vevay. In 1854, Edward paid a visit lasting over a year to his Eggleston relatives in Virginia. There he encountered a more genial mode of life, but found nothing in slavery, even in the patriarchal form practiced by his kinsfolk, to alter his deep aversion to the institution. During these years he declined several opportunities to attend college, believing, so he avowed in retrospect, that colleges were for youngsters who were unable or unwilling to educate themselves.

Already in 1852, at the age of fifteen, he had struck out for himself, clerking in a Madison grocery store, the first of a bewildering variety of occupations. Then, early in 1856, impelled by his deep-seated piety, he ventured his first sermon, at Milton, just across the river in Kentucky, with such success that the presiding elder of the Madison District licensed him to preach regularly. Almost at once an attack of tuberculosis sent him off to the rugged Territory of Minnesota, where for three months he earned his keep and restored his lungs by working in a surveyor's gang and breaking the prairie with oxen. Later in 1856 he embarked upon his ministerial duties as a Methodist itinerant in southeastern Indiana, riding circuit through the dark forest and exhorting the unregenerate to repentance. Ill health, however, obliged him the next spring to return to Minnesota.

There he spent the following nine years mostly as a parson, but occasionally sampling other means of livelihood, such as Bible agent, soap manufacturer, book peddler, insurance salesman, and exhibitor of magic-lantern slides.

Almost fortuitously Eggleston drifted into magazine writing. In 1860 he contributed to the *Ladies' Repository* in Cincinnati an essay on "Béranger, the Poet of the People," a by-product of his omnivorous reading, and in 1864 he followed it with an article on "An Incident of the Indian Massacres of 1862." This vein was a more natural one for him to exploit, and since it fell in with his desire to provide more virile literary matter for children, it led him the next year to write a series on Indian lore and pioneer life for the *Little Corporal,* a juvenile periodical published in Chicago. In 1866 he moved to the Midwest metropolis to become a member of its staff, and the following year he assumed additional duties as editor of the *Sunday School Teacher.* As though he were not sufficiently busy, he also contributed a Saturday column of local comment to the *Chicago Evening Journal* for a while, sent regular weekly articles on Western affairs to the *Independent* magazine in New York, and somehow found time also to lecture on miscellaneous topics in various parts of the country.

Well launched now on his writing career, this son of the Middle Border responded eagerly when the *Independent* in 1870 invited him to New York to join its editorial board. In that bracing literary capital, he tried his hand for the first time at fiction for adults when, after more than a year on the *Independent,* he became editor of *Hearth and Home* and serialized *The Hoosier Schoolmaster* in its pages late in 1871.

The book, faithfully depicting the Indiana of Eggleston's childhood, holds a special niche in American letters as one of the earliest novels to strike the note of realism. It sold 20,000 copies within a year and has continued to sell ever since.

Emboldened by this success, Eggleston retired from the magazine in the fall of 1872 to devote all his time to authorship. Soon he was turning out other novels treating Midwestern themes with similar fidelity: *The End of the World* (1872); *The Mystery of Metropolisville* (1873); *The Circuit Rider* (1874)—dedicated "To My Comrades of Other Years, the Brave and Self-sacrificing Men with Whom I Had the Honor to be Associated in a Frontier Ministry"—and *Roxy* (1878). Adept at keeping many balls in the air, Eggleston at the same time continued to write copiously for various periodicals, made the first of his four journeys to Europe, and took a final fling at the pulpit. He had long been cooling toward the fervid orthodoxy of his youth, and from 1875 to 1879 he presided over a creedless church in Brooklyn until his theological liberalism proved too much for powerful elements of the congregation. During the last two years of this pastorate he also collaborated with his daughter Elizabeth (Mrs. Elwin Seelye)—always known to the family as Lillie—on a set of biographies of famous Indians. This, his first excursion into American history at the adult level, sharpened his interest in the nation's past and opened his eyes to the possibilities of original work in that field.

It was during Eggleston's second visit abroad in 1880 that he decided to undertake the ambitious project of a "History of Life in the United States." Doubtless his foreign wanderings had whetted his perceptions of cultural differences between the European peoples on the two sides of the water and had made him eager to search into the underlying causes. Other factors, however, were more fundamental. As he wrote Lillie, "I am ripe for it. Everything in my life seems to have prepared me for it."

Indeed, few if any men of letters of his day had partaken so abundantly of the many-sidedness of American civilization. "In my early life," so Eggleston recapitulated to an *Outlook* interviewer upon the appearance of the first volume of the projected series, "I rapidly changed from one social environment to another"—from town to country, from a new free state to an old slave state, from the primitive Hoosier backwoods to the still rawer Minnesota frontier where the railroad had not yet penetrated and all travel was "by boat or wagon." In a very real sense, he felt that "I have known colonial life, having been among people of different manners and dialect. I can imagine in the colonies the same collision and the same contact with Indian life." Moreover, his many shifts of occupation had acquainted him with all sorts and conditions of humanity. By the same token, he had explored successive religious frontiers and hence could enter understandingly into the theological dissensions that beset the early comers to America. Finally, his change of residence to the Atlantic seaboard enabled him to view these experiences at a focal distance.

In so far as other historians influenced Eggleston, his model was the Frenchman, Augustin Thierry, whom he had first come across in an article by John Stuart Mill and then read in the original. Thierry's emphasis on the neglected role of the "popular classes" in medieval France, his concern with conveying to the reader "the atmosphere of the period," his belief that history should also be literature, all reinforced Eggleston's ideas of what he wished to do. Of his United States contemporaries, he doubtless found inspiration in the example of his old friend Moses Coit Tyler, the social historian of colonial literature; and none other than the great Francis Parkman had blessed his venture by saying, "You are the only man in America that can write a history of life in the United States; you are the only man who has seen so many forms of our life."

Actually, Eggleston's imaginative writings had also foreshadowed his plunge into history. In the preface to *The Mystery of Metropolisville* in 1873, he had demanded that novels "be the truest of books" and declared that to this end he sought to make his own stories "of value as a contribution to the history of civilization in America." And some years later, reflecting on these literary progeny, he considered that what particularly distinguished them was that the "characters were all treated in their relation to social conditions." It was not a far cry from realistic fiction to realistic history—the sort that obliged the author, as he was to say in the initial volume of his undertaking, to treat the past not "otherwise than unreverently. Here," he went on, with an eye on superpatriots and ancestor worshippers among his readers, "are no forefathers or foremothers, but simply English men and women of the seventeenth century, with the faults and fanaticisms as well as the virtues of their age."

In Eggleston's letter to Lillie in June 1880 announcing his scheme, he wrote almost lyrically, "What chapters I can write on 'Religious Life in New England,' 'The Great Kentucky Revival,' 'Flight of Emigrants Across the Mountains,' 'Indian Wars and Cabin Life in the Interior,' 'Early Fur Traders,' 'The Old Gentry in the South,' 'Social Changes of the Revolution,'" and so on. But Eggleston, even at forty-two, did not allow sufficient time to complete so formidable a task, considering the thoroughness with which he planned to do it as well as the many other activities, including the writing of three more novels, that he allowed to divert his energies. In the end he finished only two installments of the vast enterprise and did not carry it beyond the limits of the seventeenth century.

Taking advantage of his European sojourn, he hunted material in the Bibliothèque Nationale, the British Museum, and other collections in Paris and London, jotting down his findings and thoughts in two notebooks. These entries included chapter headings and tentative passages as well as subject indexes and references to further sources. Returning to New York in September 1880, he resumed his spadework, principally at the Astor Library. His snail-like progress caused him moments of despondency. "New Eng. history & all colonial history is a horrible labyrinth," he groaned in a letter to Lillie at the end of four months. In a trial draft he had set down 4,000 words on the Pilgrims in England and their flight to Holland, and he gloomily foresaw reaching "the settlement of Boston in the course of ten or fifteen years of work." By early 1882 he was pursuing his quarry in Cambridge, Massachusetts, where the learned Harvard librarian and bibliographer, Justin Winsor, helped steer his research. "The Harvard people whom I have met treat me most kindly," he reported, though some of them candidly admitted to him that until then they had never heard of him or his writings.

The next year Eggleston built a commodious field-stone library alongside his summer place at Lake George, where in due course he gathered some 10,000 volumes, eagerly scrutinizing the latest auction catalogues to acquire rare items. It proved an excellent working collection, and he found he could accomplish more there in the few months away from the heat and buzz of the city than in the whole wintertime. Through self-education he was now able to use seven languages in his researches.

Ferris Greenslet, then a young boy, remembers him at this time as a tall, slender man "with a shock of iron-grey hair and beard that stood out from the oval of his face at least five fingers' breadth in every direction, with the nose of Socrates below bright black eyes." L. Frank Tooker of the *Century Magazine* described his head, evidently Eggleston's outstanding feature, as "most leonine" with "a deep-toned voice that so easily might have become a leonine roar, but never did." The vicissitudes of an unusually varied life had in fact left him "the most genial and kindly of men."

In a third trip abroad, in 1885–86, Eggleston was elated to discover in the British Museum and the Public Record Office documents that apparently had escaped the eye of fellow historians, notably material on Bacon's Rebellion and other early Virginia developments. He also tramped in the north of England, where he visited Scrooby and Austerfield, whence the Pilgrims had set forth on their wanderings. Hearing from America that John Fiske was preparing a five-volume history of the United States, he confided in a letter to Lillie, "It will be popular, well-written, and lacking in nothing but correctness & fullness of information. I know we have no public sufficiently intellectual to justify the spending my resources on such a work as I am doing but I am compelled by internal forces to do it."

Back in his native land once more, he burrowed into the treasures of the Historical Society of Pennsylvania in Philadelphia, with his wife by his side transcribing manuscripts in "her nice antique hand." At various times he also combed the holdings of the Library of Congress, the Boston Public Library, the New York State Library at Albany, the Peabody Institute at Baltimore, and the historical societies of Massachusetts, New York, Maryland, and Virginia, besides private repositories at home and abroad. In 1889 he visited the Virginia farm where Jamestown had once stood, finding hand-wrought nails and bits of early glass, and tracing the ground plan of the first English settlement by means of the hearth bricks strewn about the field. "There is really no other way of writing vividly and familiarly," he commented in the *Outlook* interview, "except by saturating one's self."

Not long after entering upon his Sisyphean labors, Eggleston, whose habit had always been to rush into print, submitted some of his preliminary conclusions to the public. In November 1882, he began a series of thirteen articles in the *Century Magazine,* which in the next eight years treated such topics as "Husbandry in Colonial Times," "Social Life in the Colonies," and "The Colonists at Home." Early in 1883, at Justin Winsor's invitation, he read a paper on the colonial Indians before the Harvard Historical Society and was secretly irked when a member remarked that he had contributed nothing new. "It is one thing," he exploded to Lillie, "to unearth new facts as Mr. Deane does—it is quite another to see what the facts collectively amount to, & to mass them so as to carry that impression in its wholeness into the mind of the reader."

The experience may have made him resolve to dig deeper, however. In any event, such criticisms did not prevent Eggleston from being included in the notable group of scholars who assembled at Saratoga in September 1884 to organize the American Historical Association, which at once became the country's foremost agency for the advancement of research and writing in the historical field. As further evidence of the respect in which he was held, the official report of the Association's gathering in 1890 noted that "Mr. Eggleston's remarks upon various papers read in the convention were, by general consent, one of the most valuable features of the entire meeting." Nonetheless, he could never quite reconcile himself to this "new school of historians, men of large and accurate scholarship," who, thanks to German training or example, "dump the crude ore of history into ponderous sentences."

As still another offshoot of his interest in the American past, Eggleston published a school history of the United States in 1888, paralleling it the next year with one for more elementary pupils. His conscience occasionally pricked him for his distraction from his primary task, but he comforted himself with the belief that his texts would greatly improve upon the manuals currently in use. Besides, he seized the opportunity to inject his thesis of the key importance of "changes in modes of living" in "the progress of civilization." In any case he badly needed the money, and the two ventures actually yielded him the largest income he had ever enjoyed. Moreover, he discovered he had not lost face with the scholarly world, for Columbia College in 1892 invited him to deliver a series of public lectures on "The Culture-History of the American People."

"Poor history!" Eggleston lamented in a letter to Lillie in

March 1894, "no one man's life is long enough for it, certainly not the life of a sickish man like myself with a dozen other irons and no wealth to come and go on." Another embarrassment was the fact that, after nearly a decade and a half of amassing data on the first century of English settlement, he found himself with more than enough to fill two volumes on that single period alone. One student has estimated that at this rate of progress it would have required thirty-eight more volumes to carry the story to 1900. Driven by fear that "the darkness of age and death" might overtake him, Eggleston bent his energies to putting this initial material into published form.

Early in 1896, a heart ailment tempted him to go South for a rest, but, as he wrote his daughter Allegra, "only grim death itself will make me let go of my work." To render doubly certain that the volume in hand contained no errors, he engaged Victor H. Paltsits of the Lenox Library, later a scholar in his own right, to check his references, verify dates and quotations, and extend other assistance. In November the book appeared under the title *The Beginners of a Nation, a History of the Source and Rise of the Earliest English Settlements in America with Special Reference to the Life and Character of the People* and the half-title *A History of Life in the United States.* It bridges the years from the origins of Jamestown to about 1650 when, as the author held, "The compactness of English settlement and the prolific increase of English people decided the fate of North America."

After a much-needed but quick vacation at Old Point Comfort, Virginia, Eggleston returned to his toils, though "a kind of pen-paralysis" slowed his pace for a time. Finding it necessary to eke out his previous researches, he spent the

months from April to September 1897 delving in the libraries
of New York as well as in his Lake George collection, then
hied off for a protracted sojourn in Washington to run down
additional sources. "Nobody knows we are here," he wrote
Lillie, "and we are having a good quiet time."

Ill health, now further complicated by failing eyesight,
continued to plague him—he lost ten pounds during his
Washington stay—and he dolefully informed Lillie early in
1899 that his work was creeping "on all fours." By keeping
doggedly at it, however, he finished the second volume in
November of the following year. To this new portion of *A
History of Life in the United States* he gave the arresting title
*The Transit of Civilization from England to America in the
Seventeenth Century.* Unlike the first volume, it covers the
full span to 1700 except for Pennsylvania and the Carolinas,
which he optimistically reserved for later treatment. Inasmuch as the book deals with a wholly different kind of
subject matter, it possesses a completeness which enables
it to stand alone.

Of the two works, *The Beginners of a Nation* received
greater critical acclaim at the time. It was better constructed,
and, what probably counted for more, it treated thoughtfully
and luminously what was currently accepted as the orthodox
content of history. The author's principal concern was with
the English background of colonization, the hardships of the
early settlers, their theological doctrines and schisms, and
the peopling of new colonies from the older ones. Though
deploring a "paroxysm of citations," Eggleston came close to
committing the offense by amplifying many of his points in
"Elucidations" at the end of each chapter, where, however,
they could easily be ignored.

Herbert L. Osgood's review in the *American Historical*

Review reflected the general academic reception. While he denied that the volume offered many unfamiliar facts or a "distinctly new point of view," he praised Eggleston's delineation of men and events as "realistic" and termed his style of writing as "of such beauty and force as to make the book at once a history and a contribution to literature." This was no slight accolade from a professionally trained scholar who within a few years was himself to produce a monumental treatise on the legal and institutional aspects of seventeenth-century America.

The Transit of Civilization, on the other hand, was a trail-breaking book, dealing with material hitherto off the beaten track. Of contemporary writers in America, Henry Adams had made a bow to social and intellectual aspects of the past by opening his *History of the United States during the Administrations of Thomas Jefferson and James Madison* with six acute chapters of that nature and then happily forgetting all about the matter until his four concluding chapters eight volumes later. Somewhat closer to Eggleston's conception was John Bach McMaster, who began publishing his *History of the People of the United States from the Revolution to the Civil War* in 1883 and had produced five portly installments of the full set of eight before Eggleston brought out his *Transit of Civilization*.

Eggleston, however, had preceded McMaster in the field of social history with the first of his articles on colonial life in the *Century Magazine*; and, in any event, the two men addressed themselves to quite different stages of American development: one, the period of infancy; the other, that of young manhood. But what was more significant, they held very different ideas of how to evoke the past. McMaster generally sought to let the facts speak for themselves, and his unadorned account often reads like a poorly digested notebook. To an inquirer he tartly remarked, "It is not the business of the historian to be a philosopher." And despite the implications of the word *People* in the title of his work, he gave nearly three-quarters of his space to politics, diplomacy, and war.

Eggleston, who took even greater care than McMaster to authenticate his data, considered that the historian should seek to clothe the bare bones with the flesh and blood of interpretation. The historian, he believed, should try to look beneath and behind the facts, to penetrate to "the history that underlies history." The resulting interpretation should arise out of the student's complete identification with the age, but must not preclude him from utilizing such insights as were afforded by the perspective of his own day. Eggleston, moreover, deliberately played down the role of government in society as actually wielding less influence than a multitude of more urgent concerns of life.

As the name suggests, *The Transit of Civilization* centers on the "mental furniture" the English newcomers carried with them to America and the modifications wrought by wilderness conditions. In a wide-ranging survey, Eggleston considers such aspects of life as the colonists' scientific conceptions, their belief in an ever-present invisible world (which tended to be as real to them as the material world), their medical notions and practices, their religious and moral outlook, the persistence of class distinctions in law and custom, the popular distrust of lawyers, the neologisms and other changes in English speech, the modes of education and the "literature below literature that has to do with the hopes and fears, the beliefs and aspirations of uncritical people." While noting that "men may live at the same time without being intellectual contemporaries," he stresses the fact that even the better informed shared much of the credulity of the rank and file. Some of them indeed lent it the high sanction of their erudition. Eggleston again appended "Elucidations" to his chapters to provide significant supporting data.

This second volume of A *History of Life in the United States* nonplused the learned reviewers. Barrett Wendell, a literary scholar and author of a biography of Cotton Mather, passed judgment on it in the *American Historical Review*. After his well-known manner, he cavalierly pronounced it the product of intellectual indigestion induced by too much browsing in libraries; but despite this and other animadversions, he nevertheless granted that "it really points the way to a kind of American history which in time may flood our past with revivifying light."

Charles M. Andrews, who would presently rival Osgood as an authority on colonial America, greeted the work in the *Political Science Quarterly* with similar mixed feelings. With good reason he, like Wendell, accounted it a bundle of essays rather than a unified whole; and while saying he considered these disquisitions "interesting and readable," he chided the author for inaccuracies concerning the English antecedents of certain colonial land and educational practices. Obedient to the historical canons of the time, he barely mentioned Eggleston's discussions of pseudo-science, medical customs, intellectual concerns, and the like, which made up two-thirds of the book, though he cautiously surmised they "may be thoroughly sound and scholarly."

'Upon further reflection, Andrews several years later referred again in much the same manner to the "valuable chapters on out-of-the-way subjects."

Today, however, with our different criterion of the scope of history, the essence of Eggleston's achievement may be said to lie in his discerning accounts of these very "out-of-the-way subjects," no longer considered freakish and off center. Though scholars since his time have piled up detailed studies of many of the same themes, Eggleston's pioneering effort still shines through with a special glow of its own. From this longer perspective, for example, the late Carl Van Doren, American historian and man of letters, termed the work "erudite, humane, and graceful"; Ferris Greenslet, the biographer, has called it the best of all of Eggleston's many writings, "a learned, vividly written, yeasty book"; and Michael Kraus, weighing the two Eggleston volumes in his *History of American History*, has declared, more re-strainedly, that they are still informative, better written than most historical treatises, and "not as well known as they should be."

Eggleston delivered his valedictory to the historical pro-fession in December 1900 in his presidential address to the American Historical Association, which he was too ill to present in person. He chose as his title "The New History," and in a somewhat disjointed discourse that betrayed his declining powers he reiterated the convictions that had served as the guiding star of his scholarly labors. Paying tribute to Thierry, Michelet, Macaulay, Green, and other European historians for their attention to the common life, he decried "drum and trumpet history" as outmoded and unworthy of the serious student and pleaded instead for a "history of culture, the real history of men and women." He died two years later on September 2, 1902.

But neither Eggleston's example nor that of McMaster wrought any immediate transformation in American historical writing. The grip of political and military history continued too strong in academic groves to be easily dislodged. It was not until the 1920's that the thirteen-volume cooperative *History of American Life*, breaking sharply with the older point of view, began publication and that Charles and Mary Beard brought out their *Rise of American Civilization*, with many other students also turning to the field. A full generation after Eggleston's pioneering achievement, his vision of a "New History" thus came at last to fulfillment.

3 An American Historian Looks at Science and Technology

"History, as generally written, is but an account of the wars and contentions by which dynasties have striven for the mastery of nations. It imparts little or no information in respect to the social conditions or material progress of the people themselves ... Inasmuch, however, as that the nature, the institutions, and the administration of the American nation are different from all others, so must its history be in an entirely different style ... If we have no Alexander, or Caesar, or Bonaparte, or Wellington, to shine on the stormy pages of our history, we have such names as Franklin, Whitney, Morse, and a host of others, to shed a more beneficent lustre on the story of our rise. The means by which a few poor colonists have come to excel all nations in the arts of peace, and to astonish the people of Europe with their achievements through the development of their inventive genius, are true subjects for a history of the United States."

This passage has an authentically modern ring, but actually it appeared in the preface of a collaborative work entitled *Eighty Years' Progress of the United States,* published in

Reprinted from *Isis*, XXXVI (Oct. 1946), 162–166.

1866. Though American historians were put this early on notice, in the eighty years since they have nevertheless continued for the most part to celebrate wars and political contentions—the Caesars and Wellingtons rather than the Franklins and Morses. The additions to our knowledge of science and technology have come largely from other sources, two in particular, either from specialists in the various branches of science or from that breed of authors called popularizers. Those who wrote with expert understanding generally talked above the heads of lay readers, while the popularizers, seeking romance and drama in every new conquest of Nature, generally overplayed the facts or garbled the underlying principles. Both sets of writers, moreover, have tended to look at their theme with blinders, failing to correlate scientific achievement with the broader movements of history—as though the investigator or inventor lived and labored in a social vacuum.

Finally, it should be noted that the bulk of this literature deals with technology or applied science, very little of it with theoretical or pure science. To be sure, the Americans, a practical-minded people, have scored most heavily in the applied field, preferring what they term useful research to useless research. But neither this fact nor the inherent difficulty of elucidating the abstruse justifies the failure to portray adequately the developments in pure science. It hardly needs to be said that so-called useless research often turns out in the end to be the most useful kind, for it constitutes a seedbed of endless utilitarian applications. Furthermore, as the United States has matured as a nation, it has contributed ever more importantly to science and technology at the theoretical level. The four-volume history of American science, now being planned by the American Council of Learned Societies, will, if carried out, go far toward filling this gap.

Professional scholars have been slow to study the progress of science and technology, partly because of their traditional penchant for political history, and partly because, even with the rise of social and intellectual history, they have been daunted by the unfamiliar and formidable subject matter. At certain points, it is true, they have touched upon epoch-making mechanical inventions which had self-evident economic consequences, but these occasional references fall far short of depicting the pervasive and continuing role of science in all ranges of American life. For this more comprehensive task most historians have felt inadequate because their specialized training did not fit them for it.

How is this barrier to be surmounted for the future? How can a program of graduate study be designed to accomplish for scholars of the next generation what has been lacking in the preparation of our own? The difficulties are many. On the one hand, professors of history must surrender jealously guarded vested interests in order to make room for the new type of subject matter. On the other hand, their colleagues from the laboratory must cooperate by packaging their wares for a new type of customer. Since the historical student is not planning to become a specialist in any scientific field, his needs call for a different kind of instruction. As I see it, the emphasis should be placed on the methods and unifying elements of all science, the differentiating principles which have brought about increasing fragmentation and the historic discoveries that underlay the pivotal advances. To the extent that the study focuses on the United States, it will be necessary further to separate the American strands from the world web of science.

This is doubtless a counsel of perfection, and while we await Utopia, much cries to be done. The historian, even when insufficiently informed as to the data of science and technology, can often perceive social implications and inter-relations which specialists in those branches are unaware of or disregard. Here, in fact, lies the peculiar function of the historian: not so much to write the internal history of science as to trace the external connections of science and society. This relationship works both ways. Sometimes society moti-vates scientific discovery. Sometimes a new advance of science motivates social change.

Instances abound of the creative role of social conditions. As the old saying has it, necessity is the mother of invention. Benjamin Franklin in devising the famous fireplace stove explained that his attention had been directed to the need of a fuel-conserving burner by the growing scarcity and ex-pense of wood as the forests were cut down. The invention of the cotton gin represented a different sort of necessity. This appliance might have been contrived much earlier than it was, for it involved very simple mechanical prin-ciples; but, as every student knows, it was not till the 1790's that the demands of the English textile industry revealed what a gold mine lay in short-staple cotton if it could be properly cleansed for the overseas market. A Connecticut schoolmaster sojourning on a Georgia plantation supplied the answer. A generation later, when Westerners were turn-ing from subsistence tillage to commercial agriculture, the difficulty of securing hired hands called into being all the basic modern labor-saving farm implements: the steel plow, the reaper, the thresher, and the rest. As American life grew more urbanized and complex, social incentives operated to yet different ends. It would be pointless to multiply cases, but suffice it to say that the great growth of cities after the Civil War brought forth in quick succession the elevated railroad, the cable car, and the trolley car as solutions for the problem of traffic congestion, and also begot America's unique architectural innovation, the skyscraper. The influence of war in stimulating science and technology is so fresh in our minds as to require no comment except perhaps to remark that every major American war has had this effect and, further, that the results have appeared not only in death-dealing weapons and explosives, but also in notable gains in sanitation, medicine, and surgery.

While these and countless other instances support the adage that necessity is the mother of invention, the historian is obliged to demur that the expected pregnancy doesn't always ensue. In pure science, where intellectual creativeness is the analogue of technological invention, the investigator tends to pursue the bent of his curiosity without reference to time and place. It would be difficult, for example, to correlate the evolutionary theory with any crying social need of Darwin's day. Even in applied science the cause-and-effect relationship frequently fails to work. Christopher Columbus stood in desperate want of a steamship when undertaking his famous voyage; he would have been still better served by an airplane. The Indians could have saved their continent from the white man by developing the atomic bomb.

The point is not merely that some ages and peoples are more mechanically minded than others, but, more important, that most great inventions rest upon a cumulative series of subsidiary inventions. Technological discovery proceeds by progressive steps, and it seldom occurs that a single individual can skip several of these stages to achieve the final goal. Once the stationary steam engine was perfected, it was possible to plan to hitch it to a boat, but Columbus' contemporaries could not reasonably have taken this giant leap into the future. Even with the prerequisite knowledge available, the urgency of a want may not produce the looked-for results. America's vast distances clearly called for the steam locomotive, but actually it was the "tight little island" of Britain that invented it. In this case, however, we know that John Stevens and other Americans were already struggling with the problem and were on the point of succeeding when George Stephenson anticipated them.

It is also true that motives not related to social need have sometimes sired inventions. There are cases on record of mechanisms born long before their time, which later had to be reinvented. Here individual genius operated according to its own internal logic. In other instances high-powered advertising stimulated a public demand which would not otherwise have existed. It might almost be said in such cases that invention is the mother of necessity. In recent years the profit motive has operated in this regard with increasing effect and has been a potent makeweight for technological progress.

Like other monistic interpretations in history, the concept of social compulsion as the wellspring of technological change must be used with caution, but, when so applied, it is a rewarding tool of analysis. It not only accounts satisfactorily for the significant goals of invention, but also goes far toward explaining the phenomenon, already referred to, of different minds working independently at the same time on the same invention. Though England lacked America's reasons for a steam railway, she had urgent reasons of her own, notably the need to transport cheaply and quickly the bulky commodities of her factories and mines. A later and more striking case of parallel effort in the two countries is the separate discovery of the so-called Bessemer process of making steel. Still others are the steamboat and the dual discovery of the principle of electromagnetic induction.

Within the United States itself the outstanding illustrations include the reaper and the telephone, possibly also the telegraph, the sewing machine, and the airplane. These occasions of multiple discovery would seem to constitute proof positive of the workings of social necessity; yet in some equally noteworthy instances the connection is far from clear. Why, for example, did a Boston dentist and a rural Georgia physician independently originate the use of ether as an anesthetic? What special conditions in the 1840's, common to New England and the Deep South, necessitated this conquest of pain? Such apparent exceptions the careful historian must take into account, but they should not shake his faith in the usual relationship of events.

In considering the impact of society on science, it should not be forgotten that science acts with reciprocal impact on society. A stock example of history textbooks is that of the cotton gin. This instrument, by rendering cotton culture profitable in the interior South, rejuvenated the dying institution of slavery, ensured its extension throughout the section, and thereby set the stage for the Civil War. Another favorite instance is the part played by the railroad in speeding Western settlement and, especially, its role in binding

East and West by ties of mutual interest in time for them to present a united front to Southern secession. These two illustrations, when placed in juxtaposition, are instructive. In the first instance science functioned as a divisive factor politically; in the second, as a nationalizing factor. In neither case was the remoter outcome envisaged when the mechanism was devised. The inventor in accomplishing an immediate purpose loosed a stream of influences that ramified in unpredictable directions. An impersonal force, science operates on human affairs with unforeseen and often unforeseeable effect. For this if for no other reason it challenges the historian's most thoughtful attention.

The point may be further underscored by reference to some less obvious examples. Charles Goodyear's discovery of the secret of vulcanized rubber prepared the way for numerous unexpected applications. On the one hand, the new substance provided the necessary insulating material for the future age of electricity and also the tires which would hasten the coming of the bicycle and the automobile. On the other hand, vulcanized rubber had a profound effect on human health, ranging in use from the nipple on the infant's nursing bottle to the hot-water bag of the aged invalid. In the form of raincoats and overshoes it offered protection against common colds and rheumatism as well as against more fatal disorders such as pneumonia and influenza. Undoubtedly it was an important element in increasing the life span of the American people. Yet so unschooled are historians of science in reckoning with influences outside their narrow confines that no treatise on medicine has yet admitted Charles Goodyear to the roll of great healers of mankind.

A final example may well center on the lengthening span

of human existence, to which allusion has just been made. Without discussing the many factors that were responsible, the promise of life at birth increased from around thirty-five years in 1789 to about forty years in 1855 and to approximately sixty-five years at the present time. Nobody, so far as I know, has ever attempted to translate these juiceless abstractions into their social and intellectual significance. With an expected stay on earth of but thirty-five or forty years, a man saw time in a very different perspective from today. By eighteen or twenty he had lived half his life and should have attained the same relative position in the world as a person of thirty-two or thirty-three at present. This circumstance sheds light on the fabulous accomplishments of young people in those days: the youthful captains of merchant vessels and privateers; boys and girls marrying in their teens; George Washington holding public office as county surveyor at the age of seventeen; Alexander Hamilton addressing a patriot mass meeting at seventeen and becoming General Washington's aide at twenty; David G. Farragut starting as midshipman before the age of ten. One sees that the framers of the Constitution acted with characteristic conservatism in restricting membership in the House and Senate to persons of twenty-five and thirty and reserving the presidency for patriarchs of thirty-five.

But the whole time scale changed with the progressive prolongation of life after the Civil War. Youth needed no longer to shoulder the burdens of manhood. Boys now had ample leisure for play and slow maturing, for getting eight or twelve years of education, even in many cases for going to college and spending additional time in studying for a profession. Child labor fell increasingly into disrepute, while

73

legislative provision for child welfare became a major concern of society. It would take someone wiser than I to decide whether the modern accent on youth has not involved losses as well as gains, but there can be no doubt that there has resulted a significant reorientation of American life.

History, if written with a due appreciation of the role of science and technology, should have the useful effect of bridging the gap which in academic life too often separates those who study Nature from those who study human nature and society. If a scientific colleague of mine is to be believed, the college curriculum consists of the natural and unnatural sciences. If the person to whom he addressed this remark is to be believed, the distinction lies between the social and antisocial sciences. In support of this latter view a recent writer on higher education maintains that in the modern university the laboratory specialist alone lives in an ivory tower, indifferent to the tumult of events and a consistent foe of reform and change. To the extent that this may be true the layman is puzzled since the very essence of science and technology is experiment and growth. The answer, of course, lies in the fact that to the scientist's way of thinking social experimentation is not experiment at all but a misapplied figure of speech. A social experiment takes place under uncontrolled conditions, and because of the intrusion of numerous imponderables the results cannot be verified by repetition. Long ago Aristotle realized that science in this exacting sense cannot be applied to human affairs, that on the contrary such studies as history, economics, and sociology rest necessarily upon thoughtful observation.

Nevertheless the scientist, like his lay fellows, lives in a world where to stand still is to move backward, where intolerance of governmental and social change may invite disaster. And the scientist himself has been perhaps the chief contributor to this dizzy tempo of development. Can he then safely step aside and let the forces he has invoked work out their will blindly? Must he instinctively reject the fumbling, trial-and-error efforts of government to adjust society to the advances of science and technology? While not all scientists have been so minded, the examples of those who have are many and conspicuous. The historian by offering a truer picture of the past place of science may help to correct their vision. The invention of the atomic bomb seems also to be contributing to the same end. The international band of chemists, physicists, and engineers who created this terrible engine of destruction can hardly dodge the responsibility of trying to shape the kind of society that can be trusted with its use. This attitude may in turn foster a keener awareness of the implications of science for other affairs of life. In the end, we may hope, the natural and social sciences, each contributing to the wisdom of the other, will stand united in forwarding the common welfare of this nation and the world.

4 Political Mobs and the American Revolution, 1765–1776

Mass violence played a dominant role at every significant turning point of the events leading up to the War for Independence. Mobs terrified the stamp agents into resigning and forced a repeal of the tax. Mobs obstructed the execution of the Townshend Revenue Act and backed up the boycotts of British trade. Mobs triggered the Boston Massacre and later the famous Tea Party. The last disturbance, however, goaded the long-suffering Parliament to harsh retaliation, and this legislation, known ever since as the Intolerable Acts, provoked the colonists first to armed resistance and then to revolution. But even at this climactic stage of the controversy civilian mobs behind the lines systematically intimidated Tory opponents, paralyzing their efforts or driving them into exile.

This quick résumé presents a bald contrast to the traditional picture of a dignified movement of protest stemming from lofty constitutional principles and directed by men of the signal stature of James Otis, John Adams, John Dickin-

Reprinted from *Proceedings of the American Philosophical Society*, XCIX (Aug. 30, 1955), 244–250.

son, and Thomas Jefferson.[1] The point, of course, is that the patriot movement comprised diverse elements and motives, and that a posterity, grateful for the end result, has preferred to remember only the more genteel aspects. Suffice it to say, however, that a Tory commentator on the eve of the final break with England spoke out of fullness of knowledge when he asserted that "mobs were a necessary ingredient" in the mode of opposition.[2]

I

These outbreaks consisted of two general kinds: those deliberately engineered in advance by the Whig leaders and those that were spontaneous explosions. But, whatever their origin, they furthered patriot purposes in several essential ways. They highlighted grievances as mere words could never have done; they struck terror into the hearts of British adherents; and, as notably in the case of the Boston Massacre, they fashioned folk heroes out of street loafers and hoodlums.

Three examples will illustrate the calculated use of violence. The first consisted of the mobs throughout the continent which in 1765 ousted the stamp distributors before the Stamp Act had time to go into effect. What General Gage

1. For a historiographical explanation of this attitude, see S. G. Fisher, "The Legendary and Myth-Making Process in Histories of the American Revolution," *Proc. Amer. Philos. Soc.*, LI (1912), 53–76. As Fisher remarks in conclusion, "The real Revolution is more useful and interesting than the make believe one."

2. "Massachusettensis" (Daniel Leonard) in the *Massachusetts Gazette and Boston Post-Boy*, Dec. 19, 1774.

remarked of the situation in New York held equally true of all the other colonies. "The Plan of the People of Property," he informed the Ministry, "has been to raise the lower Class to prevent the Execution of the Law," and he opined that many of the instigators had themselves shared in the riots.[3] In Boston the Whig politicians took little pains to conceal their participation, for some forty substantial citizens, thinly disguised in the trousers and jackets of mechanics, headed the marchers who wrecked the stampmaster's abode.[4] Lieutenant Governor Thomas Hutchinson, one of the victims of the attendant commotions, has described the local chain of command. The "rabble," he said, took their cue from "a superior set consisting of master-masons, carpenters, &c.," who in turn took theirs from a merchants' committee in certain matters and from the "mob-high eloquence" of the town meeting in still others.[5] If this evidence be regarded as prejudiced, John Adams' diary supplies ample corroboration.

A second outstanding example of premeditated lawlessness was the burning of the British revenue schooner *Gaspee* near Providence, Rhode Island, at midnight of June 9, 1772. John Brown, one of the town's leading merchants, not only organized the destruction ahead of time but personally took

3. Letter to H. S. Conway, Dec. 21, 1765, in Thomas Gage, *Correspondence with the Secretaries of State*, ed. C. E. Carter (New Haven, 1931–33), I, 78. For the situation generally in the colonies in this respect, see William Gordon, *The History of the Rise, Progress, and Establishment of the Independence of the United States* (London, 1788), I, 199, and Edmund S. and Helen M. Morgan, *The Stamp Act Crisis* (Chapel Hill, 1953), 180–187.

4. Thomas Hutchinson, *The History of the Province of Massachusetts Bay* (London, 1828), III, 120–121.

5. J. K. Hosmer, *The Life of Thomas Hutchinson* (Boston, 1896), 103–104.

part in it.[6] But the most notable instance was the Boston Tea Party late in the following year.[7]

Over a space of six weeks before the event, the town meeting and various unofficial gatherings, augmented by people from neighboring communities, had protested the importation of dutied tea by the monopolistic East India Company. When in due course the vessels arrived and the Crown authorities refused to allow them to depart without payment of the hated tax, Samuel Adams, jumping to his feet in the densely packed Old South Church, gave the prearranged signal: "This meeting can do nothing more to save the country." At once a war whoop at the door started a lurking band of make-believe Mohawk Indians to Griffin's Wharf, where they cast the 342 chests into the harbor. A crowd on shore looked silently on. History has never beheld a more superbly disciplined mob. Despite the intense excitement the vandals hurt no person aboard and were so respectful of private property that they even replaced a broken padlock.[8]

II

By contrast were the countless self-willed mobs. A notorious early instance was the pillaging of Lieutenant

6. J. R. Bartlett, *A History of the Destruction of His Britannic Majesty's Schooner Gaspee* (Providence, 1861), 17, 19, 23; J. B. Hedges, *The Browns of Providence Plantations: Colonial Years* (Cambridge, Mass., 1952), 209–210.

7. A. M. Schlesinger, *The Colonial Merchants and the American Revolution* (New York, 1918), 281–290; George Bancroft, *History of the United States* (Boston, 1834–74), VI, 472–478; Edward Channing and A. C. Coolidge, eds., *Barrington-Bernard Correspondence* (Cambridge, Mass., 1912), 294–302.

8. F. S. Drake, ed., *Tea Leaves* (Boston, 1884), lxv, lxviii.

Governor Hutchinson's mansion in Boston in August 1765 during the Stamp Act disorders. Not content with gutting the structure from ground to roof, the "hellish crew" scattered abroad Hutchinson's historical papers and the manuscript of the second volume of his *History of Massachusetts Bay*.[9] Even more alarming was the so-called Battle of Golden Hill in New York in January 1770. This was the climax of a long series of street brawls between the populace and the redcoats that had been going on ever since the troops were stationed there for purposes of imperial defense at the close of the French and Indian War. In this culminating affair the soldiers fought back with bayonets and cutlasses, killing one of the crowd and wounding others.[10]

But the pre-eminent affray with the military was the set-to on King Street in Boston some weeks later. A British garrison had been sent to the Massachusetts capital two years before following a particularly daring riot over the customhouse seizure of John Hancock's sloop *Liberty* for alleged smuggling. Bad blood had quickly developed between the soldiers and "the inhabitants of the lower class," who openly insulted the intruders, beat them up in the dark streets, and haled them into court on every possible excuse.[11] Popular resentment mounted dangerously when a customs informer accidentally killed a boy while firing into a threatening mob. When the funeral was held, a great throng ostentatiously

9. Hutchinson to Richard Jackson, Aug. 30, 1765, in *Publications of the Colonial Society of Massachusetts*, XXVI (1924–26), 33. Hosmer, *Hutchinson*, 351–362, gives a detailed inventory of the losses.

10. H. B. Dawson, *The Sons of Liberty in New York* (New York, 1859), 112–118.

11. The quoted phrase is John Adams' in his *Works*, ed. C. F. Adams (Boston, 1850–56), II, 230.

escorted the remains to the cemetery in imitation of a recent turnout in London for a child murdered during a riot in St. George's Field. The demonstration was, as Hutchinson bitterly remarked, designed further "to raise the passions of the people." [12]

Soon afterward, on the night of March 5, 1770, a file of regulars, provoked beyond endurance, shot into a crowd of their tormentors, slaying five and injuring others. The tragedy was purely an affair of the moment, but the Whig chieftains, quick-wittedly capitalizing on the propaganda possibilities, at once labeled it the "Boston Massacre" and acclaimed the fallen—whose very names were unfamiliar to most of the townsfolk—as martyrs to the cause of American liberty. Not all the patriots, however, agreed. Two of the most respected, indeed, John Adams and Josiah Quincy, Jr., acted as legal counsel for the soldiers at their trial and secured their acquittal of the charge of murder. It is also significant of the sober second thought of the inhabitants in general that in the midst of the furor they elected Adams for the first time to the legislature.[13]

III

Political mobs, though long prevalent in England and never more rampageous than during the 1760's, had hitherto

12. Hutchinson, *Massachusetts Bay*, III, 269–270.

13. Adams, *Works*, II, 230–236. The essential documents for the whole episode may be found in Frederic Kidder, ed., *History of the Boston Massacre* (Albany, 1870).

been rare or unknown in America.[14] The absence of deep-seated and irremediable class divisions plus the eagerness of the colonial legislatures to espouse popular rights probably account for the difference. But now, with the issues involving a distant and uncontrollable Parliament, mobs roared into action on the slightest pretext all the way from New Hampshire to Georgia. Though the coastal cities set the pace, inland towns and villages were seldom far behind.

The Crown officials stood well-nigh helpless before the anarchy. The colonial law-enforcement agencies usually winked at the outbreaks, and if the culprits were brought into court, the juries quickly cleared them. This is not surprising, because sometimes both the magistrates and individual jurors had themselves joined in the disturbances and, in any event, they did not dare risk the consequences of defying community sentiment; in New England indeed the town meetings actually elected the jurors. General Gage reported from New York that "the Officers of the Crown grow more timid, and more fearfull of doing their Duty every Day." And in similar strain Governor Hutchinson declared of his plight during the opposition to the East India Company shipments, "There was not a justice of peace, sheriff,

14. Benjamin Franklin wrote from London in 1768, "I have seen within a year riots in the country about corn; riots about elections; riots about work-houses; riots of colliers; riots of weavers; riots of coal-heavers, riots of sawyers; riots of Wilkesites; riots of government chairmen; riots of smugglers; in which custom-house officers and excisemen have been murdered, and the King's armed vessels and troops fired at." W. V. Wells, *The Life and Public Services of Samuel Adams* (Boston, 1865), I, 228–229n. For a historical account of this aspect of the 1760's, see W. E. H. Lecky, *A History of England in the Eighteenth Century* (New York, 1878–90), III, 98–99, 143–148, 163–164, and, for an earlier period, Max Beloff, *Public Order and Popular Disturbances, 1660–1714* (London, 1938), chap. 2.

constable, or peace officer in the province, who would venture to take cognizance of any breach of law, against the general bent of the people."[15]

Behind this "bent of the people" lay the fact that the masses perceived nothing morally wrong in nullifying attempts to enforce legislation which they considered oppressive and to which they had never consented. Few Americans could accept the British view that the tumults were criminal proceedings, and those who did so ordinarily kept silent out of a prudential regard for their own persons and property. There was, to be sure, though mainly outside Massachusetts, a strong vocal reaction to the Boston Tea Party, as an uncalled-for deed of destruction, but this vanished when Parliament overreached itself by passing the Intolerable Acts.[16]

It is also to be noted that a singular self-restraint characterized the frenzies, for the participants invariably stopped short of inflicting death. They trusted to horror rather than to homicide. Though occasionally brandishing cutlasses and muskets, they typically employed less lethal weapons like clubs, rocks, brickbats, and clods of dung. "In truth," wrote the English historian, Lecky, in the 1880's generalizing upon this curious phenomenon, "although no people have indulged more largely than the Americans in violent,

15. Letter to Lord Barrington, July 22, 1769, in Gage, *Correspondence,* II, 518; Hutchinson, *Massachusetts Bay,* III, 437.

16. Schlesinger, *Colonial Merchants and the American Revolution,* 289–300, 304, 309–311. Even within Massachusetts the town meeting of Freetown shortly after the drowning of the tea denounced the "Spirit of Anarchy, Disorder and Confusion prevailing in some Parts of this Province" and bade its member of the Assembly to put an end to "all such riotous and mobish Proceedings." *Boston Evening-Post,* Feb. 7, 1774.

reckless, and unscrupulous language, no people have at every period been more signally free from the thirst for blood, which in moments of great political excitement has been often shown both in England and France."[17] This forebearance doubtless made it easier for the more law-abiding Whigs to condone the outbreaks but it afforded cold comfort to the victims, who never knew when a mob, fortified perhaps with alcoholic as well as patriotic spirits, might overstep the bounds.

Still the greater opprobrium, that of actually taking lives, fell alone on the "British tyrants" and their hirelings. Considering the repeated provocations the wonder is that they did not do so more often, but this fact naturally failed to impress the colonists. The Massachusetts patriots, taking political advantage of the most fatal of these incidents, annually commemorated the Boston Massacre with awesome ceremonies. On each anniversary the bells of the town tolled at intervals during the day, and at night lighted transparencies near the site of the bloodshed displayed tableaux of the "murderers" and the dead, with perhaps a symbolic America trampling a supine redcoat under foot. Sometimes an exhortation in verse pointed up the moral, such as the screed beginning:

17. Lecky, *England in the Eighteenth Century,* III, 401. William Gordon in his *Rise, Progress, and Establishment of the Independence of the United States,* I, 321, published a few years after the war, states that, "in all my researches, not an instance has occurred to me of the mob's having been the death of a single individual." "Novanglus" (John Adams) in the *Boston Gazette,* Feb. 13, 1775, and "Lucius" in the *Massachusetts Spy,* March 9 of the same year, earlier boasted of this record. There were, however, some near-fatalities, notably the shooting of a soldier in the sequence of incidents eventuating in the Boston Massacre, and the wounding of the commander of the *Gaspee.*

> Canst thou, Spectator, view this crimson'd Scene,
> And not reflect what these sad Portraits mean?
> Or can they slaughter'd Brethren's guiltless Gore,
> Revenge, from Year to Year, in vain implore?[18]

The crowning event was the declamation by a well-known figure, who pulled out all the stops to do full justice to his theme. To quote one of the orators,

> Words can poorly paint the horrid scene—defenceless, prostrate bleeding countrymen—the piercing agonizing groans—the mingled moan of weeping relatives and friends—these best can speak, to rouse the luke-warm into noble zeal; to fire the zealous into manly rage, against the foul oppression of quartering troops, in populous cities, in times of peace.[19]

These addresses, besides electrifying those within earshot, reached a far larger public in printed form and, as John Adams tells us, they "were read, I had almost said by everybody that can read, and scarcely ever with dry eyes."[20] The yearly orations continued—though necessarily outside Boston while the British held hostile possession—until the town authorities in 1783 substituted the celebration of the Fourth of July.

While the rioters avoided fatalities, they had no compunctions about wantonly destroying property, mauling the

18. *Boston Gazette,* March 8, 1773.
19. Dr. Benjamin Church, 1773, in Hezekiah Niles, ed., *Principles and Acts of the American Revolution,* rev. ed. (New York, 1876), 37, in which work can be found the texts of all the orations, on pp. 17–79.
20. Letter to Jedidiah Morse, Jan. 5, 1816, in Adams, *Works,* X, 203.

unfortunates, tar-and-feathering them, and lynching them in effigy. The tar brush was the favorite discipline for those of low degree. The mob after applying a "suit of the modern mode" carted the victim through the town as an object lesson to others as well as himself.[21] Squire M'Fingal's ordeal in John Trumbull's mock epic of a Massachusetts Tory hardly exaggerates genuine occurrences.[22] In one affair the vigilantes even set fire to the feathers.[23]

Hanging in effigy was reserved for offenders of higher station. Even though this form of retribution did not harm the flesh, it was probably no easier on the spirit. Royal governors, stampmasters, revenue collectors, contumacious importers, tea consignees, and the like suffered this indignity, sometimes in company with their official superiors in London— Lord Bute, George Grenville, Lord North, and so on—or with their alleged infernal chief, the devil. After the passage of the act in 1774 legally establishing Roman Catholicism in the province of Quebec, the Pope sometimes joined the cast of characters, thus symbolizing the people's religious as well as political bias. Indeed, the overzealous townsfolk of Newport, Rhode Island, on one occasion displayed two Popes.[24] The accepted ritual was to exhibit the grotesque figures for some hours, then carry them through the streets to the gallows or to a funeral pyre. As in the case of tar-and-

21. The quoted expression is from the *Boston Evening-Post,* June 25, 1770, and the *New-Hampshire Gazette,* Jan. 20, 1775. In a similar facetious spirit a group at Falmouth, Casco Bay, announced the appointment of a "Committee for Tarring and Feathering" consisting of "Thomas Tarbucket, Peter Pitch, Abraham Wildfowl, David Plaister, Benjamin Brush, Oliver Scarecrow and Henry Hand-Cart." *Massachusetts Spy,* Feb. 24, 1774.

22. *M'Fingal* (many editions), Canto Third.

23. E. A. Jones, *The Loyalists of Massachusetts* (London, 1930), 243.

24. *Newport Mercury,* Nov. 7, 1774.

feathering, the proceedings, whether or not intimidating the persons intended, vividly advertised the enormity of their misconduct to the public.

IV

The representatives of the Crown continually sent home pathetic accounts of their helplessness in the face of these excesses, but the London authorities were too far away and too preoccupied with their own pressing affairs to give the matter systematic attention. Francis Bernard, Hutchinson's predecessor as governor of Massachusetts, complained that "the indifference which has been shown in England to the checking the Demagogues of America for so long a Time has at length so effectually discouraged the Friends of Government, that they have been gradually falling off, 'till at length the Cause is become desperate."[25]

Yet even when the imperial government sought to lend a hand, as it did from time to time, the results were invariably disappointing. Upon the repeal of the Stamp Act the Ministry, at the behest of the House of Commons, instructed the colonial governors to require the legislative assemblies to indemnify all persons who had lost property in the disorders; but only three provinces responded. Of these, Maryland alone voted full damages; New York recompensed one of the two major sufferers but not the other; and Massachusetts after stalling for fifteen months reimbursed Hutchinson for his looted mansion, but only on condition of a general

25. Letter to Lord Barrington, July 30, 1768, in *Barrington-Bernard Correspondence*, 170.

amnesty for all mob participants throughout the province during the troubles.[26]

Three years later, in 1769, the government moved to prevent the thwarting of justice by biased juries in the prosecution of rioters. With this object chiefly in mind Parliament proposed that colonists charged with treasonable behavior be conveyed to England for trial under an old statute of Henry VIII;[27] and in retribution for the *Gaspee* destruction in Rhode Island in 1772, the Ministry set up a royal commission to do just that. Though the tribunal conducted its inquiry on the spot and fully a thousand people must have known the perpetrators, it could not obtain sufficient evidence to apprehend a single suspect.[28] The proceeding only resulted in sending a flame of indignation through the colonies.

Nor did the presence of British troops in New York and Boston, the major storm centers, have the desired effect. On the contrary, the enforced association, irksome to both parties, merely intensified the friction that normally exists between garrisons and the civilian population. To the townsfolk the "Bloody Backs" were visible reminders of "English

26. *Annual Register for the Year 1766* (London, 1767), 46; Horatio Sharpe to Hugh Hamersley, Dec. 8, 1776, in Sharpe, *Correspondence*, ed. W. H. Browne (*Archives of Maryland*, XIV [Baltimore, 1895]), III, 358; Alice M. Keys, *Cadwallader Colden* (New York, 1906), 330–331; E. F. Brown, *Joseph Hawley* (New York, 1933), 107–110; L. H. Gipson, *The Coming of the Revolution* (New York, 1954), 165–169. The Privy Council disallowed the Massachusetts enactment because of the rider, but not in time to stop the payment of £3,194 from being made.
27. Gipson, *Coming of Revolution*, 192–193.
28. Eugene Wulsin, "The Political Consequences of the Burning of the Gaspee," *Rhode Island History*, III (1944), 1–11, 55–64; W. R. Leslie, "The Gaspee Affair: A Study of Its Constitutional Significance," *Mississippi Valley Historical Review*, XXXIX (1952–53), 233–256; Bartlett, *Destruction of His Britannic Majesty's Schooner Gaspee*, 55–140.

tyranny," hence proper objects of verbal and physical harassment; and not unnaturally the soldiers returned these attentions in kind. The Battle of Golden Hill and the Boston Massacre were merely extreme examples of the explosive outcome.

It was a preconcerted riot, however, not a spontaneous disturbance, that finally drove Britain to drastic punitive action. The Intolerable Acts, passed in retaliation for the Boston Tea Party, permanently deprived the entire province of cherished democratic privileges and closed the port of Boston to seaborne commerce until the East India Company should be reimbursed and the King be otherwise convinced that the Bostonians henceforth would be law-abiding. Parliament further took away from the Whig-controlled town meetings the right of choosing juries and gave it to the sheriffs, who were creatures of the Crown-appointed governor; and, to make assurance doubly sure, it provided that anyone accused of murder while quelling an outbreak might be tried in another colony or in England.[29]

This stringent legislation, precipitated by a particular act of mobbing, dealt with conditions that had actually been long out of hand. But, however warranted the measures appeared from the meridian of London, they outraged the colonists' sense of fair dealing by ignoring the distinction between innocent and guilty and indicting a whole people for the sins of a few. Parliament thereby exercised an authority far more ominous to popular liberties than taxation without representation or invidious trade regulations.

Had the Americans through the years pursued only lawful methods of opposition, the crisis could not have arisen, and

29. 14 George III, c. 19, c. 39, c. 45.

the mother country would have avoided this naked display of power. Now, even though Massachusetts was the one province struck at, the Ministry flung down a challenge which the other colonies dared not ignore, since none knew when its own turn might come. Within a few months the First Continental Congress assembled, and a train of events began which led to Lexington and Concord and onward to independence.

V

When the troubles began some ten years before, no one could have foreseen this outcome, and few if any would have desired it. Virtually everyone believed that the difficulties could be and should be adjusted within the framework of the Empire. Hence opinion had been divided, even among the patriots, as to the use of violence. Men like James Otis and John Dickinson earnestly counseled against it as not only unworthy of the cause but as being far more likely to alienate England than to induce concessions.[30] Moreover, as General Gage observed at the time of the Stamp Act, political mobs tended to become mobs with a roving commission. For this reason, he informed his London superiors, the well-to-do citizens, who had unleashed the terror, had drawn back in dismay when the rioters began pursuing objects of their own.[31]

30. For Otis, see Richard Frothingham, *Life and Times of Joseph Warren* (Boston, 1865), 38–39n; and for Dickinson, his *Writings*, ed. P. L. Ford (*Memoirs of the Historical Society of Pennsylvania*, XIV [1895]), I, 323–325.

31. Letter to H. S. Conway, Dec. 21, 1765, in Gage, *Correspondence*, I, 78–79; similarly, Cadwallader Colden to Sir Jeffrey Amherst, June 24, 1766, in Colden, *Letter Books* (*Collections of the New-York Historical Society*, X [1877]), II, 111.

Gouverneur Morris, on the opposite side of the political fence, struck a similar note when he wrote somewhat sardonically at a later juncture that "the heads of the mobility grow dangerous to the gentry ... The mob begin to think and to reason. Poor reptiles! it is with them a vernal morning; they are struggling to cast off their winter's slough, they bask in the sunshine, and ere noon they will bite, depend upon it."[32] When the First Continental Congress assembled, it also registered disapproval of "routs, riots, or licentious attacks upon the properties of any person whatsoever, as being subversive of all order and government."[33] By that time, however, the damage had already been done—and the benefit reaped. It is likewise revealing that even in the instance of the Boston Tea Party none of the actors publicly admitted complicity until more than half a century had elapsed.[34]

This ambivalent attitude toward mass violence cannot better be illustrated than in the case of that sterling patriot, John Adams. Deeply versed in jurisprudence, and law-abiding by nature, he, unlike his kinsman Samuel, shrank from the use of force and thoroughly distrusted nameless men whose brains were in their biceps. Instrumental in drawing up a protest against the Stamp Act for his home town of Braintree, he decided after perceiving its effects on the public of Massachusetts that "a man ought to be very cautious what kinds of fuel he throws into a fire." Yet, when

32. Letter to John Penn, May 20, 1774, in Peter Force, comp., *American Archives*, 4th ser. (Washington, 1837), I, 342–343.
33. The Congress acted by reaffirming resolutions first adopted by a patriot convention in Suffolk County, Massachusetts. Continental Congress, *Journals*, ed. W. C. Ford and others (Washington, 1904–37), I, 36.
34. Drake, *Tea Leaves*, xcii.

popular uprisings throughout the continent killed the law, he wrote exultantly in his diary: "So triumphant is the spirit of liberty everywhere. Such a union was never before known in America."[35]

His doubts returned, though, when the dispute with Parliament presently resumed; and as attorney for the soldiers in the Boston Massacre, he sternly warned his countrymen against "the dangers of various kinds which must arise from intemperate heats and irregular commotions."[36] The Tea Party, however, once more reversed his attitude, causing him to exclaim, "This is the grandest event which has ever yet happened since the controversy with Britain opened. The sublimity of it charms me!"[37] In his emotional commitment to the American cause Adams had now arrived at a point where he consciously distinguished between good mobs and bad ones. "These private mobs," he wrote his wife, "I do and will detest," referring to "the insolent rabble" acting "in resentment for private wrongs, or in pursuance of private prejudices and passions." But, even so, he told her, he could approve of the political variety only "when fundamentals are invaded, nor then, unless for absolute necessity, and with great caution."[38]

But already he was beginning to wonder whether mob rule was not in any case preferable to abject submission to Britain (as though there were no middle ground), asking, "Will not Parliamentary taxation, if established, occasion vices, crimes, and follies infinitely more numerous, dan-

35. Adams, *Works*, II, 153, 173.
36. *Ibid.*, II, 236.
37. *Ibid.*, IX, 333.
38. John and Abigail Adams, *Familiar Letters*, ed. C. F. Adams (Boston, 1875), 13.

gerous and fatal to the community?"[39] Soon, under the pen name of "Novanglus," he was proclaiming this opinion in the press and charging the Crown officials with accoutering their more deadly mobs "with red coats, fuzees and bayonets." Then, going the whole distance, he learnedly justified disturbances and insurrections for the public good by citing the writings of Grotius, Pufendorf, Le Clerc, Sidney, and Locke. Adams' own conclusion was that, when rulers transgressed the laws of God and man, it followed that "seditions, tumults and wars, are justified by the laws of God and man."[40]

Under the relentless impact of events the reluctant revolutionist thus came at last to vindicate unreservedly the strategy of direct action which he had once so deeply deplored. Even more illuminating was Adams' considered view of this phase of his young manhood long afterward when he was bowed with years. Nothing had offended his sense of orderly government so much as the popular fevers that had begotten the Boston Massacre. Yet half a century later, as he pondered the episode, he handsomely attested that "the blood of the martyrs, right or wrong, proved to be the seeds of the congregation."[41]

That, too, if more broadly applied to the revolutionary violence, must be the judgment of history.

39. *Ibid.*, 14.
40. *Boston Gazette*, Feb. 13, 27, 1775.
41. Letter to Jedidiah Morse, Jan. 5, 1816, in *Works*, X, 203.

5 The Lost Meaning of "The Pursuit of Happiness"

Probably no historical expression is more familiar to Americans than "the pursuit of happiness," immortalized by the preamble of the Declaration of Independence. Yet it has puzzled many that life and liberty should be pronounced by the great document as "unalienable rights" of "all men" but not happiness—only the pursuit of it. It is worth asking, however, what Jefferson and his associates on the drafting committee really meant by the famous phrase. Able scholars have repeatedly examined the meaning of the text as a whole, but none has given attention to this particular wording.[1]

Reprinted from *William and Mary Quarterly*, 3d Ser., XXI (July 1964), 325–327.

1. Among the more notable book-length studies are Carl Becker, *The Declaration of Independence, a Study in the History of Political Ideas* (New York, 1922); Julian P. Boyd, *The Declaration of Independence: The Evolution of the Text as Shown in Facsimiles of Various Drafts by Its Author* (Washington, 1943); Edward Dumbauld, *The Declaration of Independence and What It Means Today* (Norman, Okla., 1950); Herbert Friedenwald, *The Declaration of Independence, an Interpretation and an Analysis* (New York, 1904); and John H. Hazelton, *The Declaration of Independence, Its History* . . . (New York, 1906). Howard Mumford Jones, *The Pursuit of Happiness* (Cambridge, Mass., 1953), deals with the meaning of the word "happiness," especially as later interpreted, but not with that of "pursuit," which alone concerns the present essay.

What, then, was the import of the term "pursuit" in the minds of the framers of the Declaration? Did it signify merely the pursuing or seeking of happiness, as is conventionally assumed, or was it used in a different sense, as when we today refer to the pursuit of law or the pursuit of medicine? According to the *New English Dictionary* it has borne both meanings since at least the sixteenth century.[2] Obviously the distinction is a vital one, for, if the common supposition is mistaken, it follows that the historic manifesto proclaimed the *practicing* rather than the *quest* of happiness as a basic right equally with life and liberty. For evidence of this usage contemporary with the Anglo-American dispute the *New English Dictionary* cites a letter of Edmund Burke in 1774 in which he wrote, "Your constitution of mind is such, that you must have a pursuit."[3]

In this sense of the actual practicing—and in no other, so far as I have found—the concept also appeared in patriot writings during the controversy. Thus James Otis in *The Rights of the British Colonies Asserted and Proved* (Boston, 1764) affirmed that the duty of government is "above all things to provide for the security, the quiet, and happy enjoyment of life, liberty, and property."[4] More categorically, Josiah Quincy, Jr., in his *Observations on the Act of Parliament Commonly Called the Boston Port-Bill* (Boston,

2. The alternative definitions there given are: "The action of pursuing, chasing, or following, with intent to overtake and catch," and "The action of following or engaging in something, as a profession, business, recreation, etc.," James A. H. Murray, ed., *A New English Dictionary on Historical Principles* (Oxford, Eng., 1888–1925), VII, 1636.

3. *Ibid.*

4. James Otis, *Some Political Writings*, in Charles F. Mullett, ed., *University of Missouri Studies*, IV (Columbia, Mo., 1929), 309.

95

1774) avowed that the proper object of civil society is "the greatest happiness of the greatest number,"[5] and James Wilson in his *Considerations on the Nature and Extent of the Legislative Authority of the British Parliament* (Philadelphia, 1774) asserted that "the happiness of the society is the *first* law of every government."[6] Likewise John Adams in his *Thoughts on Government* (Philadelphia, 1776) declared that "the happiness of society is the end of government."[7] In short, none of these spokesmen of the American cause thought of happiness as something a people were entitled simply to strive for but as something that was theirs by natural right.

As though to make this conception unquestionably clear, the revolutionary Virginia Convention's memorable Declaration of Rights on June 12, 1776, particularized it as the "pursuing and obtaining" of happiness.[8] The language was that of George Mason, Jefferson's long-time friend whom he described in his autobiography as "a man of the first order of wisdom among those who acted on the theatre of the Revolution."[9] It is unlikely that in drawing up the Declaration of

5. Josiah Quincy, *Memoir of the Life of Josiah Quincy, Junior, of Massachusetts, 1744–1775*, 2d ed. (Boston, 1874), 323.

6. Bird Wilson, ed., *The Works of the Honourable James Wilson . . .* (Philadelphia, 1804), III, 206.

7. Charles Francis Adams, ed., *The Works of John Adams . . .* (Boston, 1850–56), IV, 193.

8. Helen Hill, *George Mason, Constitutionalist* (Cambridge, Mass., 1938), 136. This wording may have seemed the more necessary because John Locke, whose writings were a major source of patriot inspiration, had used the expression, "the pursuit of happiness," in the sense of "pursuing." For examples see Herbert L. Ganter, "Jefferson's 'Pursuit of Happiness' and Some Forgotten Men," *William and Mary Quarterly*, 2d Ser., XVI (1936), 564.

9. Hill, *George Mason, Constitutionalist*, 152.

Independence shortly afterward for the Continental Congress he did not take Mason's phrasing into account.

Why he determined upon his own more concise rendering we do not know, but doubtless he deemed the added words sheer excess baggage. As John Adams, one of his colleagues on the drafting committee, said, Jefferson was noted for "a happy talent of composition" and "peculiar felicity of expression." [10] In any case the latter part of the sentence containing his formulation stated explicitly that it is a government's duty to the governed "to effect their safety and happiness." The extraordinary thing is that through the years the two parts of this sentence have not been read together. Adams, who had flatly declared a few months before that "the happiness of society is the end of government," found no fault with Jefferson's version, though he did not hesitate to suggest changes elsewhere in the document.[11]

In view of these circumstances the conclusion seems inescapable that the long-standing misinterpretation of "the pursuit of happiness" should at last be corrected and the history books be rewritten to restore to the celebrated phrase its more emphatic meaning.

10. Letter to Timothy Pickering, Aug. 6, 1822, in C. F. Adams, ed., *Works*, II, 513–514*n*.

11. Becker, *Declaration of Independence*, 136–138, 152–155.

6   Was Olmsted an Un-
biased Critic of the South?

Frederick Law Olmsted, a Connecticut-born farmer of Staten Island, traveled through the South in 1852–1854, reporting his findings in newspaper articles and then later in a trilogy of volumes: *A Journey in the Seaboard Slave States* (New York, 1856), *A Journey through Texas* (1857), and *A Journey in the Back Country* (1860). These books in turn were condensed into *The Cotton Kingdom* (2 vols., New York, 1861). No writings on the pre-Civil War South are better known to historians or have been so influential in fashioning the picture we have today of plantation life and slavery. Did Olmsted merit this trust? Granted that no human being can be wholly objective, did he carry prejudices with him into the South which made it impossible for him to be a fair observer? The critical question, of course, is his attitude toward Negro slavery; and from this standpoint it is fortunate that ample evidence is available as to what he thought of the system before, during, and after his travels.

Reprinted from *Journal of Negro History*, XXXVII (April 1952), 173–187. "Was Olmsted an Unbiased Critic of the South?" was incorporated, in slightly different form and with the additional section on "The South through Olmsted's Eyes," into the author's introduction to Olmsted's *The Cotton Kingdom*, copyright 1953 by Alfred A. Knopf, Inc. The section on "The South through Olmsted's Eyes" is reprinted here with the publisher's permission.

I

Writing to his father in 1846, six years prior to his first trip, he avowed, "The tyranny of priests and churches is as great a curse to the country and the world as negro Slavery." He had evidently been pondering John C. Calhoun's justification of the institution, for he added to his friend, Charles Loring Brace, that the South Carolinian's arguments had persuaded him "that Slavery is not the greatest sin in the world—that a Slaveholder may be a conscientious Christian." Olmsted, in fact, could not "believe Slaveholding to be *either* an unforgiveable sin or a 'beneficial Institution sanctioned by God.'" Though he felt Calhoun to be wrong, "he *may* be right. God knows, I honestly believe he may be right."[1] Nevertheless he was troubled that the Southern students whom he had known at Yale "do not seem to have a fundamental sense of right," having "no power of comprehending a hatred of slavery in itself," and ascribing Northern objections merely to a "regard for self-interest."[2] At the same time he deplored the blackguarding of slaveholders in the press, "exasperating them—Acting as if we hated them as much as we did their doctrines." The proper way was to "*reason* with them as though *we might be* the mistaken ones, for truly I think in my heart we *may* be."[3]

1. Olmsted to his father, Aug. 12, 1846, and to Brace, March 22, 1846. These and later letters are cited from the Olmsted Papers in the Library of Congress unless otherwise indicated.

2. Olmsted to Frederick J. Kingsbury, June 1846, in Broadus Mitchell, *Frederick Law Olmsted, a Critic of the Old South* (Baltimore, 1924), 38.

3. Olmsted to Brace, May 27, 1846.

Notwithstanding such inner doubts he wrote his father at an early stage of the fight in Congress over the Wilmot Proviso that he hoped the admission of Texas with slavery meant that Oregon and California—other recent or prospective acquisitions—would be without. "If," he said, "we can but secure that before the lines are irretrievably drawn —then at least I hope it will be North and freedom vs. South and slavery," thus opening the way for gradual emancipation and the colonization of the freedmen in Africa.[4] This solution of the problem was one which was increasingly to engage Olmsted's attention. A year later, in 1847, he dismissed a recent declaration of principles by the Liberty party as too Garrisonian in spirit and "far from convincing." By contrast, he described himself as a lukewarm Whig, a choice he justified on the score that the Whigs were the more national-minded of the two major parties.[5]

During a trip abroad in 1850 he resented the view he often heard expressed in England that the North, except for "a few martyrs, called abolitionists," was as responsible for slavery as the South, but in almost the same breath he declared the British practice of primogeniture "more naturally abhorrent and wrong" than Negro bondage. He counseled the Southerners to send some lecturers to England to counteract abolitionist misrepresentations.[6] Returning home amid the "fearful reaction" in the North to the new Fugitive Slave Act, he blamed both sections for the uproar, but thought the "free principles" of Northerners would succumb

4. Olmsted to his father, Aug. 12, 1846.
5. Olmsted to Brace, Sept. 20, 1847, and to Kingsbury, Sept. 23, 1847.
6. Olmsted, *Walks and Talks of an American Farmer* (New York, 1852), 215, 221.

to the danger of losing Southern trade. "Money," he said, "is at the bottom of the sin on both sides."[7] In the 1852 campaign he supported the Whigs who, like the Democrats, pledged continuance of the Compromise of 1850, though he declared privately that he "would take in a fugitive slave and shoot the man that was likely to get him. On the whole I guess I represent pretty fairly the average sentiment of good thinking men on our side."[8]

II

Olmsted correctly said of himself that when he undertook his first Southern trip shortly after the election "few men could have been so little inclined to establish previously formed opinions as I was."[9] To an extraordinary degree he had kept his mind free from the passions which had for so long inflamed his countrymen's thinking on the slavery issue. As a believer in democracy he could not approve of human bondage in principle, but he recognized the "clear constitutional right" of the Southern states "to continue their peculiar institution, as it is, and where it is," and he regarded abolition as no more immediately practicable than the abolition of penitentiaries and hospitals.[10] He could even cry, "Who are we to condemn our brother? . . . No slave freezes to death for want of habitation and fuel, as have men in Boston . . . Remember that, Mrs. Stowe. Remember that, indignant sympathizers."[11] At the most, as has been seen, he

7. Olmsted to Brace, Nov. 12, 1850.
8. Olmsted to Kingsbury, Oct. 17, 1852.
9. *Back Country,* vi.
10. *Seaboard Slave States,* x; *New York Times,* Feb. 13, 1854, p. 2; *Back Country,* vi.
11. *New York Times,* April 8, 1853, p. 2.

desired to stop the institution from spreading farther—he "would rather the Union be dissolved" than have this occur[12] —and he considered it a dirty business for Northerners to return escaped Negroes.

Then and later, he viewed slavery, per se, as "an unfortunate circumstance for which the people of the South were in no wise to blame," and held that "much mischief had resulted from statements and descriptions of occurrences which were exceptional, as if they were ordinary phenomena attending slavery." On the contrary, he believed the whites to be discharging an "unenviable duty" at much personal inconvenience, and that the gains to the Negroes from enforced association with a superior race "far outweighed the occasional cruelties, and other evils incidental to the system." Determined to examine conditions "carefully and fairly," he would also do so "cheerfully and kindly," seeking for "the causes and extenuating circumstances, past and present, of those phenomena which are commonly reported to the prejudice of the slaveholding community; and especially of those features which are manifestly most to be regretted."[13]

Though Olmsted adhered to some of these ideas for over twelve months of his wanderings, rejecting counter evidence as probably atypical, he felt obliged in the end to abandon most of them.[14] As he confessed at the close of his wayfaring, "I saw much more of what I had not anticipated and less of what I had, in the Slave States, than, with a somewhat

12. *Ibid.*, Feb. 13, 1854, p. 2.

13. This paragraph rests upon the *Seaboard Slave States*, ix, and on the *Back Country*, vi and 70–71. The last reference recurs in the *Cotton Kingdom*, II, 219–220.

14. *Back Country*, 71 (*Cotton Kingdom*, II, 220).

extended traveling experience, in any other country I ever visited."[15] His new convictions, though, did not render him dogmatic or denunciatory, or lead him to withhold facts from his readers that did not document his views. And even as late as 1860 he still felt that the dominant race was caught in a historical trap and that, everything considered, the "subjection of the negroes" to the "mastership of the whites" was "justifiable and necessary."[16]

By the same token Olmsted continued to decry the course of the Northern abolitionists, whose high moral tone ignored the practical difficulties of emancipation. He likewise deplored their loathing of Southerners as individuals and their willingness to imperil the very survival of the Union for their cause. In his view they were as wrongheaded as those at the other pole of the argument who stood for "hopeless, dawnless, unredeeming slavery."[17] "The extremists of the South," he said, "esteem their opponents as madmen, or robbers," while "The extremists of the North esteem the slave-holders as robbers and tyrants, willfully and malevolently oppressive and cruel."[18] In his "Letter to a Southern Friend," which prefaced the *Journey through Texas*, he denied, however, that any "formidable number" of North-

15. *Seaboard Slave States*, 179. Though this was the first volume of the trilogy, he had completed his second and third journeys before writing it.

16. *Back Country*, viii. Despite his avowed belief in democracy he had written in the *New York Times*, Feb. 13, 1854, p. 2, "I do not consider slave-holding—the simple exercise of the authority of a master over the negroes who have so wickedly been enslaved—in itself, necessarily wrong, any more than all forcible constraint of a child or lunatic is wrong," though he added, "*Slavery as it is*, in the vast majority of cases, is shamefully cruel, selfish and wicked."

17. *Walks and Talks of an American Farmer*, rev. ed. (Columbus, 1859), 278.

18. *Seaboard Slave States*, 177.

erners wished to interfere with slavery where it was already entrenched, though perhaps half the population (of whom he was, of course, one) held it to be an evil which should not be extended elsewhere.[19] Moreover, he questioned the common Southern contention that the militancy of abolitionism had badgered the people of the slave states into a firmer attachment to the institution. That attitude he attributed, rather, to the South's increasing economic stake in the system.[20]

III

Olmsted's sojourn in Texas, though shedding no additional light on his antislavery sentiments, put them to the test of action. He and his brother John, who accompanied him, spent considerable time among the Germans in the New Braunfels district of Western Texas, between San Antonio and Austin, where the thrifty management of the settlers and their repugnance to human bondage greatly impressed the visitors. So strong was the feeling against slavery that Olmsted estimated that not more than thirty out of the nearly twenty-five thousand Germans in Western Texas owned Negroes.[21] Since Texas as admitted to the Union in 1845 exceeded in area New England, the Middle Atlantic states, Maryland, Virginia, and Kentucky combined, Congress had provided that, as the population increased, it might be divided into as many as five commonwealths with the state's

19. *Journey through Texas*, xv.
20. *Seaboard Slave States*, 283–284.
21. *Journey through Texas*, 428, 432. The account that follows rests upon *ibid.*, 434–439, and Laura Wood Roper, "Frederick Law Olmsted and the Western Texas Free-Soil Movement," *American Historical Review*, LVI (1950–51), 58–61.

consent. The possibility therefore existed that slavery might be barred from part of the broad expanse.

Dr. Adolf Douai, editor of the San Antonio *Zeitung*, whom the Olmsteds had met and admired, fronted the movement for making Western Texas into a free state; and when some of the paper's stockholders, unwilling to antagonize their Anglo-American neighbors, tried to muzzle him, he appealed in September 1854 to the Olmsted brothers, then back in New York, for a loan to enable him to continue publishing on his own. They quickly secured the money from Charles Brace, Henry Ward Beecher, and other antislavery sympathizers, helped Douai get printing equipment in New York, and drummed up subscribers for the publication. Moreover, Olmsted, besides agreeing to write a fortnightly letter for the *Zeitung*, induced the *New York Times* to publish editorials and articles to encourage Northern emigration to Western Texas. These pieces, for political reasons, intentionally side-stepped the free-soil angle for the economic advantages. Douai, however, finding the local opposition too powerful, quit the paper and the hopeless cause in May 1856 and removed to the more congenial atmosphere of Boston.

Meanwhile Olmsted had become involved in a similar campaign to keep slavery out of Kansas, an issue much more prominent in the national eye. The dispute over this region, growing out of the passage of the Kansas-Nebraska Act in 1854, had reached the stage of bloodshed, and Olmsted, with the assistance of Horace Greeley, David Dudley Field, and others, raised funds to provide the free-state party in Kansas with its first cannon. The howitzer arrived in time to help beat off the attack of the proslavery forces on Lawrence in

December 1855.[22] In his "Letter to a Southern Friend" in the *Journey through Texas* Olmsted bitterly denounced the "fraud and violence" of the slavery elements in both Kansas and Texas, and in the "Introduction" to a book on the Kansas situation by a *London Times* reporter he flayed the pro-Southern course of the federal administration as well.[23]

Olmsted's deeper concern, however, remained with Western Texas, perhaps because he felt that the North was already sufficiently stirred up over "Bleeding Kansas," which the newly formed Republican party made one of its major issues in the 1856 campaign. His volume on Texas, appearing a few months after the election, did not openly urge Northern emigration to the Lone Star state, but that was its logic, and he took every occasion to use the book as a promotional tract. Though the prospect of carving a free state out of Texas was no longer bright, he nevertheless believed that free labor, by demonstrating its superior efficiency in the growing of cotton, would lead to the curtailment or abandonment of slave labor.[24] Hearing that some of the Kansas free-soilers were hoping to "take Western Texas next," he offered Edward Everett Hale of the New England Emigrant Aid Company a hundred copies of his book at cost to send among them. He gave others to leading antislavery men like Theodore Parker and John Greenleaf Whittier, and even

22. J. B. Abbott, "The Abbott Howitzer—Its History," Kansas State Historical Society, *Transactions*, I–II (1881), 221–226.

23. *Journey through Texas*, xix; T. H. Gladstone, *The Englishman in Kansas; or Squatter Life and Border Warfare* (London, 1857), "Introduction" and chap. xxvi (both by Olmsted). Gladstone arrived in New York in January 1856, and after traveling in the Lower South went by way of Missouri to Kansas in the spring.

24. *Back Country*, 184 (*Cotton Kingdom*, II, 102).

circulated selected pages of the work to New England news-paper editors.[25]

With still less result he tried to stimulate English migra-tion to the region, on the plea that the greater productivity of free labor would relieve British fears that the Southern output of cotton would not keep abreast of the mounting industrial demand in that country.[26] Besides writing to J. T. Delane of the *London Times* and other English acquaintances, he appealed directly to the Cotton Supply Associations of Manchester and Liverpool, buttressing his arguments with copies of his book and offering to present the case to them in person. Nor did the outbreak of the war exhaust his interest in Western Texas. Joining with the Massachusetts textile manufacturer Edward Atkinson and others, he urged that an "army of colonization" be dispatched to detach the area from the Confederacy and so replenish the North's shortage of cotton. The ill-starred attack on Galveston at the close of 1862 was the sole outcome.

IV

These concerns and activities in no sense belied the care-ful distinction Olmsted invariably drew between slavery as a pre-existing institution and its transplantation to fresh soil.

25. Roper, "Olmsted and the Western Texas Free-Soil Movement," 61–62.

26. This account is based on *ibid.*, 62–65; P. W. Bidwell, ed., "The New England Emigrant Aid Company and English Cotton Supply Asso-ciations: Letters of Frederick L. Olmsted," *American Historical Review*, XXIII (1917–18), 114–119; H. F. Williamson, *Edward Atkinson* (Boston, 1934), 5–8; and G. W. Smith, "The Banks Expedition of 1862," *Louisiana Historical Quarterly*, XXVI (1943), 341–360.

Despite his firsthand acquaintance with the aggressive nature of the slavocracy, he continued to look upon Negro servitude where it was already rooted as "an entailed misfortune which, with the best disposition, it might require centuries to wholly dispose of."[27] In sympathizing with the white man's plight, however, he did not ignore the black man's, for the system in his judgment misdirected and debased the laborer's ambition, withholding "all the natural motives, which lead men to increase their capacity of usefulness to their country and the world."[28] Yet he opposed instant emancipation by federal edict, not only on constitutional grounds, but also because he doubted whether it would accomplish what was expected: "An extraction of the bullet does not at once remedy the injury of a gun-shot wound; it sometimes aggravates it."[29]

Olmsted's own solution was gradual manumission by action of the slaveholders themselves.[30] This he regarded as not improbable, once they faced up to the economic drawbacks of the system. As steps toward the goal, an owner should systematically foster habits of self-reliance in his thralls and permit them to buy their liberation by accumulating financial credits as payment for their toil. Even so, Olmsted was not starry-eyed about the outcome. He did not believe the ex-slaves would ever "become Teutons or Celts," rather that they would be "of tenfold more in value to the commonwealth than they are." He foresaw a difficult race problem, however, when enough Negroes should be freed,

27. Gladstone, *Englishman in Kansas*, xxxvii.
28. *Seaboard Slave States*, 711 (*Cotton Kingdom*, II, 251).
29. *Back Country*, vii.
30. *Seaboard Slave States*, 443–445 (*Cotton Kingdom*, I, 255–258); *Back Country*, viii–ix, 482–483.

and hence hoped that "something" would "force, or encourage and facilitate, a voluntary and spontaneous separation" of the two peoples at that time. Olmsted was obviously indebted to Jefferson's scheme of gradual emancipation in the *Notes on Virginia* (1785), and he attributed certain features of his plan to the self-liberation law in Cuba and the reformatory system of some of the British penal colonies.[31] He was undoubtedly also acquainted with the program of the American Colonization Society.

In the *Back Country,* in the summer of 1860, he presented his proposal with a fresh note of urgency, declaring that it was the only means of averting an eventual military clash between the sections. So long as human bondage endured, he said, the very existence of the North organized on a basis of voluntary labor would be a standing threat to the servile system, and the South's increasing demand for federal legislation to protect and nurture slavery would sooner or later, perhaps "ten or twenty years hence," impel the free states to call a halt on further concessions. Though he did not deny the South's abstract right to secede when that moment should come, he warned that the North would take up arms to prevent it.[32]

V

Far more swiftly than he had anticipated, the exodus of states began after Lincoln's election in the autumn; and Olmsted in December wrote to Charles Brace, who reflected

31. He discusses Jefferson's plan in the *Seaboard Slave States,* 261–265, and refers to the two others on 445–446.

32. *Back Country,* 445–457 (*Cotton Kingdom,* II, 361–363), 459, 481.

a temporary sentiment in abolitionist circles that the South's departure was good riddance, that "my mind is made up for a fight. The sooner we get used to the idea the better, I think."[33] In his opinion the preservation of the Union was now the overriding consideration. As he had told an intimate some years before, "I am tremendously patriotic . . . it's the strongest principle in my nature."[34] Hence, with the onset of the war, he forsook his cherished plan of gradual emancipation. Discussing "The Present Crisis" in the *Cotton Kingdom*, he declared that the "first *shotted*-gun that was fired" at Fort Sumter had outmoded it, convincing him beyond the shadow of a doubt that "the one system or the other is to thrive and extend, and eventually possess this whole land." Either we must "subjugate slavery, or be subjugated by it."[35]

Nonetheless, the fate of the Southern Negroes under the altered conditions was never far from his thoughts. He did not share Brace's expectation that they would voluntarily rise against their masters, but he called on the government to seize strategic points to which they could escape and thus help demoralize the South. He also believed they should be enlisted as soldiers.[36] But the increasing certainty that the government would abolish slavery gave him pause, for it was not easy to shed long-held convictions as to the race's unpreparedness.[37] To him they were still "half savage Africans." He voiced the fear, after six months or so of the

33. Mitchell, *Olmsted*, 54.

34. Olmsted to F. J. Kingsbury, Sept. 23, 1847.

35. *Cotton Kingdom*, I, 3–4.

36. Olmsted to Brace, Oct. 4, 1862; "Yeoman" in *New York Times*, Dec. 4, 1861, p. 2.

37. The account that follows is based on Mitchell, *Olmsted*, 57–58, and his quotations from Olmsted's correspondence.

struggle, that "the slaves will get emancipated long before we are in a condition to deal with them decently in any other way than as slaves." With this in mind he urged the federal authorities to provide constructive employment for freedmen in districts occupied by the troops, and he even toyed with the idea of himself taking over the "management of a large negro colony." After the Emancipation Proclamation on January 1, 1863, he participated actively in the discussions that led Congress in March 1865 to create the Bureau for the Relief of Freedmen and Refugees. Unfortunately, this agency accomplished only a small part of what Olmsted had desired.

VI

In a backward look a quarter of a century later, Olmsted took stock of the social and economic changes which defeat had forced upon the South, and with characteristic frankness confessed wherein his own judgment had been amiss. He noted that after the war thoughtful Northerners, even though they believed that "the great mass of the freed-men were as yet ludicrously unfitted to be trusted with the ballot," had nevertheless favored enfranchisement on the ground that the vote would protect the Negroes against the danger of "some sort of quasi-slavery" after the withdrawal of the Union troops. In line with such views, Congress had made Negro suffrage central to its Reconstruction program, but he himself had thought this unwise.

"If I could," he wrote, "I would have secured to the freed-men the full rights of intending citizens yet unnaturalized" and so have made "political equality a privilege to be earned." He still hoped that the Southern states would enact a literacy test for voting, applicable, however, to both races. Notwithstanding such reservations he freely admitted:

> The negroes have been doing a great deal better as freedmen than I had ever imagined it possible that they would. The whites have accepted the situation about as well as it was in human nature that they should, and we have been advancing toward prosperity and in prosperity under the new state of things at the South amazingly more than I had thought would be possible in so short a time after so great a catastrophe.[38]

VII

In the light of this inventory of Olmsted's views on the slavery question over the years, he might perhaps be charged with obtuseness to some of the moral implications of the institution, but he can hardly be accused of undue prejudice against the South. From first to last he pursued an individual course between extremes of opinion, seeking to perform a mediatorial role. He addressed himself in matter-of-fact tones to the human intelligence while voices screamed all about him. He stressed the economic aspects of slavery in

38. Letter to Thomas H. Clark, Aug. 5, 1889, reprinted in Clark's article, "Frederick Law Olmsted on the South, 1889," *South Atlantic Quarterly,* III (1904), 11–15. I am indebted to Dr. Samuel R. Spencer, Jr., of Davidson College for this reference.

his writings because that side naturally interested a man of his particular background, but he may also have felt that it afforded the best antidote to passion and unreason in both sections. If, as someone has said, a first-rate mind is one that can entertain opposing ideas and still retain the capacity to function, Olmsted amply met the specifications. While frankly expressing his own judgments—in the *Seaboard Slave States* he called himself an "honest growler"—he carefully presented the evidence from which others might draw their own conclusions. As he stated in the *Back Country*, "my first conscious purpose has been to obtain and report the facts of ordinary life at the South, not to supply arguments."[39]

It is difficult to conceive of a more objective critic of Southern life. This in fact was the almost universal opinion of contemporaneous reviewers, who characterized Olmsted's writings as "temperate," "singularly fair," "impartial," "dispassionate," "unbiased," "conciliatory," "authentic."[40] Since these commentators, however, may themselves have been swayed by antislavery predilections, the cooler judgment of historians in after years obviously merits greater weight. That verdict is equally impressive, for with few exceptions such scholars, whether of Northern or Southern

39. *Seaboard Slave States,* ix; *Back Country,* ix. Echoing Olmsted's characterization of himself, Thomas H. Clark, an Alabamian, wrote in 1904, "The South may well be grateful that this kindly, growling note-taker came amongst us." "Olmsted on the South," 12.

40. *Household Words,* XIV (Aug. 23, 1856), 138; *New Englander,* XIV (1856), 265; *North American Review,* LXXXIII (1856), 279, LXXXIV (1857), 566, XCI (1860), 571; *Atlantic Monthly,* VI (1860), 635; H. T. Tuckerman, *America and Her Commentators* (New York, 1864), 417–418. For an angry dissent by J. D. B. De Bow, see "Texas," *De Bow's Review,* XXIII (1857), 113–131.

birth, have accorded Olmsted like praise.[41] Even those who
have questioned some of his inferences have generally
trusted his factual data.[42] Olmsted, in the judgment of those
best qualified to judge, thus emerges as a disinterested and
reliable witness of conditions in the Old South. No other
contemporary observer possesses equivalent credentials.

41. A. J. Beveridge, *Abraham Lincoln* (Boston, 1928), II, 6n; P. W.
Bidwell in *American Historical Review*, XXIII (1917–18), 114; Clement
Eaton, *Freedom of Thought in the Old South* (Durham, 1930), 112; A. B.
Hart, *Slavery and Abolition* (New York, 1906), 335; H. M. Henry, *The Police
Control of the Slave in South Carolina* (Emory, 1914), 204; Richard Hof-
stadter, "U. B. Phillips and the Plantation Legend," *Journal of Negro His-
tory*, XXIX (1944), 121; J. F. Jameson in *Mississippi Valley Historical
Review*, XXXV (1948–49), 659 (letter of May 24, 1926, to A. J. Beveridge);
Broadus Mitchell, *Olmsted*, 68–70, 97–98; Allan Nevins, *The Emergence of
Lincoln* (New York, 1950), I, 203; J. F. Rhodes, *History of the United States*,
I (New York, 1892), 304n; F. B. Simkins, *The South Old and New* (New York,
1947), 498; and W. P. Trent, "Introduction," *Seaboard Slave States* (New
York, 1904), xxxv.

42. Of these dissidents, W. E. Dodd (*The Cotton Kingdom*, New Haven,
1919, p. 148) and F. L. Owsley (*Plain Folk of the Old South*, Baton Rouge,
1949, pp. 2–3) praise Olmsted's reporting of facts, but caution against the
antislavery slant of his conclusions. More extreme are U. B. Phillips who,
though constantly citing data from Olmsted, implies that he went south to
make out a case against slavery (*American Negro Slavery*, New York, 1918,
pp. 287, 293); S. B. Weeks who, emulating De Bow, finds him guilty of
"bitterness, prejudice, misrepresentation and contradictions" (J. N. Larned,
ed., *The Literature of American History*, Boston, 1902, p. 195); and J. C.
Bonner who is in agreement with both Phillips and Weeks ("Profile of a
Late Ante-Bellum Community," *American Historical Review*, XLIV,
1943–44, p. 663). Both Hofstadter and Mitchell take specific issue with
Phillips, Hofstadter holding that "a fuller and more accurate knowledge of
the late ante-bellum South can be obtained from the volumes of Olmsted
than from Professor Phillips' own writings" ("Phillips and the Plantation
Legend," 121; Mitchell, *Olmsted*, 70n, 90). "The real question is," as
Thomas H. Clark suggests in the *South Atlantic Quarterly*, III (1904), 12,
"did the writer tell the truth?" and the answer of this Southerner was:
"There is a transparent candor in every line Olmsted wrote."

Was Olmsted an Unbiased Critic of the South?

THE SOUTH THROUGH OLMSTED'S EYES[*]

Alexis de Tocqueville, traveling in the United States in the 1830's, maintained "that almost all the differences which may be noticed between the Americans in the Southern and in the Northern states have originated in slavery."[1] Olmsted, out of a much fuller knowledge of conditions, came to a like conclusion. The American, however, did not make the mistake of regarding the South as a uniform economic and social section. He was impressed not only by the contrasts between the "grand divisions of old settlement and of recent settlement," but also by the divergences between seaboard and interior, between lowlands and hill country, as well as the differences between the Gulf zone and the border states. But, though he perceived Souths rather than *the* South, he found the common denominator—the ligature binding the various parts—in the practice of human bondage. In this fundamental sense there was one South, distinct from the rest of the United States and from most of the Western world.

Slavery, as Olmsted viewed Southern life and society, everywhere determined mental attitudes, ways of living, human relations, politics, customs, manners, and laws. It enslaved the white man almost as much as the black, yielding

[*]Reprinted from Frederick Law Olmsted, *The Cotton Kingdom*, edited with an introduction by Arthur M. Schlesinger (New York: Alfred A. Knopf, 1953), xlvii–lv.

[1]. Phillips Bradley, ed., *Democracy in America* (New York, 1945), I, 365. Broadus Mitchell, *Frederick Law Olmsted: A Critic of the Old South* (Baltimore, 1924), chaps. ii–iii, compares Olmsted's observations with those of other contemporaries, foreign and domestic. For additional British commentators, consult Max Berger, "American Slavery as Seen by British Visitors, 1836-1860," *Journal of Negro History*, XXX (1945), 181–202, and Laura A. White, "The South in the 1850's as Seen by British Consuls," *Journal of Southern History*, I (1935), 29–48.

advantages to each incommensurate with the disadvantages. Olmsted rejected the idea that it was the hot weather, rather than the labor system, that accounted for the South's economic and social backwardness. Discussing this point in connection with Virginia, he noted that the most "successful and prosperous States of antiquity were of a climate warmer than that of Virginia." In fact, the protracted heat should have favored the slave states over the free states, since it lengthened the season during which the soil could be worked and reduced the cost of wintering cattle, while it also ensured the operations of manufacturing, trade, and mining against interruptions by ice and snow.[2]

Holding such views, he naturally denied the favorite Southern contention that only the African could withstand the blazing sun. On the contrary, he said, "The recent German settlers in Texas and in South Carolina, the whites on steamboats and railroads and in trade, the white workmen in New Orleans, as well as thousands of exceptional, hardworking and successful laboring Southerners, testify that the climate is no preventive of persevering toil by the white race in any part of the slave States." He further pointed out that Caucasians displayed "no lack of strength or endurance when engaged in athletic exercise which is immediately gratifying to their ambition, passions, or their tastes."[3] The aversion to manual toil arose, rather, from

2. Olmsted, *A Journey in the Seaboard Slave States* (New York, 1856), 181. It was perhaps with some malice that he quoted Dr. E. H. Barton of New Orleans to the effect that the Southern climate was much more bearable summer and winter than the Northern. Olmsted, *A Journey in the Back Country* (New York, 1860), 344 (*Cotton Kingdom*, 500). All references to the *Cotton Kingdom* are to the 1953 edition rather than to the original work of 1861.

3. *Back Country*, 298–299. For observations of similar import, see *ibid.*, 342–344, 349–350 (*Cotton Kingdom*, 497–500, 505). On the predominance

the fact that "to work industriously and steadily, especially under directions from another man," was regarded by the master race as the lot of slaves—whence came the Southern expression: "to work like a nigger."[4]

Olmsted was equally certain that the primitive manner of living—the lack of conveniences, the slovenly ways, the addiction to violence, the intellectual destitution—did not stem from frontier conditions. In the free states pioneer life was a transitional stage, a spur to improvement, something to surmount and leave behind. "The child born to-day on the northern frontier," he observed, "in most cases, before it is ten years old, will be living in a well organized and tolerably well provided community," with access to schools, churches, and printing presses, or at least be within a day's journey of them and always within reach of their influence. In the slave states, on the other hand, the rude order of existence tended to be permanent. "There are improvements, and communities loosely and gradually cohering in various parts of the South," he conceded, "but so slowly, so feebly, so irregularly, that men's minds and habits are knit firm quite independently of this class of social influences."[5]

He could not avoid the conclusion that slavery prolonged "the evils which properly belong only to a frontier." In his "Letter to a Southern Friend" he amplified the point by contrasting the rate of advance in Texas with that in Iowa,

---

of white labor in New Orleans, see the *Seaboard Slave States*, 590–591 (*Cotton Kingdom*, 233).

4. *Cotton Kingdom*, 19.

5. Olmsted, *A Journey through Texas; or, a Saddle-Trip on the South-western Frontier* (New York, 1857), xix *n*; *Back Country*, 321–325, 414 (*Cotton Kingdom*, 532–535, 554–555). See also the *Cotton Kingdom*, 17–18, 21–22.

both newly settled areas.[6] His crowning example, however, was Virginia, oldest of the slave states, where "an essentially frontier condition of society" still persisted after more than two centuries. In fact, he asserted, "Beasts and birds of prey, forests and marshes are increasing; bridges, schools, churches and shops are diminishing in number, where slavery has existed longest. The habits of the people correspond."[7]

Olmsted further insisted that the slavery system had enhanced the economic liabilities which the presence of several million Negroes undeniably created for the South. Servile labor, though sometimes profitable, had in general a blighting effect. It not only stunted the intelligence and initiative of the bondsmen, but encouraged "sogering" on the job, accounted for the shiftless poor-white class, and arrested the inflow of enterprising individuals from the North and Europe. It also depleted the soil, increased greatly the overhead costs of farming, and locked up capital that might have nourished a more diversified economic development. With handicaps like these, how could the whites hope to thrive?

> Put the best race of men under heaven into a land where all industry is obliged to bear the weight of such a system, and inevitably their ingenuity, enterprise, and skill will be paralyzed, the land will be impoverished, its resources of wealth will remain undeveloped, or will be wasted; and only by the favor of some extraordinary advantage can it compare, in prosperity, with countries

6. *Journey through Texas*, viii-xii. Though admitting that he spoke at second hand of conditions in Iowa, he went on to extend the comparison to New York, where he had personal knowledge (pp. xii–xiii).

7. *Back Country*, 292.

118

adjoining, in which a more simple, natural, and healthy system of labor prevails.[8]

As we have seen, Olmsted did not think that the magic wand of immediate emancipation was the answer. The Negroes must be helped to unlearn the bad habits which slavery had drilled into them before striking out for themselves.

Olmsted's preoccupation with the common life of Dixie opens him to the criticism that he neglected the more gracious features of Southern civilization and hence painted an unduly dark picture. He may have been anticipating this reproach when he wrote:

> Men of literary taste or clerical habits are always apt to overlook the working-classes, and to confine the records they make of their own times, in a great degree, to the habits and fortunes of their own associates, or to those of people of superior rank to themselves, of whose sayings and doings their vanity, as well as their curiosity, leads them to most carefully inform themselves. The dumb masses have often been so lost in this shadow of egotism, that, in later days, it has been impossible to discern the very real influence their character and condition has had on the fortune and fate of nations.[9]

He might have justified his attitude further by noting that, in any event, the great planters were few. Indeed, slaveholders, whether large or small, constituted but a minority of the white population—something like a quarter of the families, according to J. D. B. De Bow, Superintendent of

8. *Seaboard Slave States*, 479.
9. *Ibid.*, 214–215.

the 1850 Census.[10] Of this favored group, 26.6 percent in 1850 owned only one to ten Negroes apiece, and 51.8 percent owned more than ten but fewer than fifty apiece. That left a mere 21.6 percent to comprise the planting aristocracy; in other words, a little more than one in five masters and perhaps a twentieth of the whole white population.[11] But, of course, as a Southern historical scholar has recently said, "This small privileged class of planters tended to think of themselves as 'the South'; they confused their narrow class interests as identical with the welfare of the whole South."[12]

Olmsted, if little concerned with this exclusive element, did not ignore it. He had known and admired some of these Southern patricians at Yale, and en route to Texas late in 1853 he and John had visited one of them in Nashville. Interestingly enough, the brothers fell into a discussion with their host over whether "gentlemen in the Southern sense" were known in the free states. Olmsted, though conceding their absence, "tried to show him that there were compensations in the *general* elevation of all classes at the North, but he did not seem to care for it."[13] Again and again Olmsted made it clear in his published writings that the greatest good of the greatest number was for him the touchstone of a well-ordered society.

Nonetheless, he visited as many large estates as their proportionate number probably merited. In the *Cotton Kingdom*, for example, he describes a 2,000-acre farm in Mary-

10. *The Industrial Resources, etc., of the Southern and Western States* (New Orleans, 1852–1853), II, 108, cited in the *Back Country*, 297 (*Cotton Kingdom*, 541).

11. L. C. Gray, *History of Agriculture in the Southern United States to 1860* (Washington, 1933), I, 530.

12. Clement Eaton, *A History of the Old South* (New York, 1949), 445.

13. Letter of December 1853. Mitchell, *Olmsted*, 48.

land, nationally known for its "excellent management"; some "show plantations" in Georgia, two of which, under a single owner, employed 200 slaves; several sugar estates in Louisiana with a comparable labor force; an extensive cotton property in Texas; two others in Mississippi, with 135 and 500 blacks respectively, as well as an "opulent" plantation in Tennessee. The "most profitable estate" he saw—identified merely as on a "tributary of the Mississippi"—comprised four contiguous plantations under separate overseers bossing more than a hundred Negroes apiece.[14] He found the general manager well educated and a delightful companion and the slaves excellently cared for, many of them living in commodious cabins—though it was also on this occasion that he first saw a woman flogged.

On the basis of this sampling and of other knowledge gained at first or second hand, he arrived at certain generalizations concerning the Southern upper class. He noted a marked difference between the seaboard aristocrats and those of the newer Gulf states. Though there were fewer wealthy families in the older region, they were superior in "refinement and education." In fact, he discovered "less vulgar display, and more intrinsic elegance, and habitual refinement in the best society of South Carolina, than in any distinct class" of the North. In Mississippi, on the other hand, as in New York and Manchester, the "farce of the vulgar-rich" evidenced "the rapidity with which certain values have advanced, especially that of cotton, and, simultaneously, that of cotton lands and negroes." Even here he encountered

14. For this last instance, see the *Cotton Kingdom*, 445–460 (*Back Country*, 72–93). The estate was actually on the Red River, and the total slave population was nearly a thousand. See the *New York Times*, Nov. 21, 1853, p. 2.

men of breeding. With all his praise of the South Carolina gentry, however, they had failed to perform the function which in his judgment society had a right to expect of them. They had done little "for the advancement of learning and science, and there have been fewer valuable inventions and discoveries, or designs in art, or literary compositions of a high rank," than in "any community of equal numbers and wealth, probably in the world."[15]

In general, he felt that Southerners reputed to be worth $400,000 enjoyed fewer advantages than men with $100,000 in the older Northern states.[16] He also thought the conventional picture of "a master's occupying the position of a father toward his slaves and of the slaves accepting this relation, affectionately, faithfully and confidingly," was grossly exaggerated, being particularly improbable for practical reasons where the owner had a numerous labor force.[17] Mulling over the discussion with his Nashville friend early in his wanderings, Olmsted concluded upon further observation and reflection that "The Southern gentleman, as we ordinarily conceive him to be, is as rare a phenomenon in the South at the present day as is the old squire of Geoffrey Crayon in modern England."[18] Indeed, "there is unquestionably at this time a very much larger number of thoroughly well bred and even high bred people in the free than in the

15. *Back Country*, 27–28 (*Cotton Kingdom*, 416–417); *Seaboard Slave States*, 501–502.

16. *Cotton Kingdom*, 107. For comparable statements, see the *Seaboard Slave States*, 652, and the *Back Country*, 326 (*Cotton Kingdom*, 330, 536–537).

17. *Back Country*, 288. He saw more of this "patriarchal character" in North Carolina than in any other state, because "of the less concentration of wealth in families or individuals." *Seaboard Slave States*, 367 (*Cotton Kingdom*, 149).

18. *Back Country*, 117–118 (*Cotton Kingdom*, 476).

slave States. It is equally certain that the proportion of such people to the whole population of whites is larger at the North than the South."[19]

There are few aspects of the pre-Civil War South which Olmsted does not illumine, whether you accept his judgments at face value or not. Perhaps no vanished civilization has suffered more misrepresentation at the hands of both friend and foe. But after visiting the slave states in Olmsted's company the reader is in a position to form his own opinion. It is true that Olmsted found little to interest him in the cities, but, apart from Baltimore and St. Louis, his itinerary included all the largest ones (New Orleans, Louisville, Charleston, Richmond, Mobile, Savannah, Norfolk, Lexington, and Nashville, ranging in population according to the 1850 census from 116,000 to 10,000, in the order named), as well as many of the smaller ones. Except for a few of the major centers, he reported that half the streets were usually "tolerably good pastures, the other half intolerable cartroads," with the "majority of shops selling raisins, nailroads [iron strips to be cut into nails] and nigger cloth, from the same counter with silks, and school books and 'bitters.'"[20] He tried every possible mode of transportation and describes graphically the mean accommodations commonly afforded by the hotels and inns.

Since the South was primarily an agricultural section and he an agriculturist, he familiarized himself with a variety of rural industries—tobacco, rice, cotton, and sugar culture,

19. *Back Country*, 424 (slightly rephrased in *Cotton Kingdom*, 563). See also, to like effect, the *Back Country*, 391–400 (*Cotton Kingdom*, 517–520, 542–545). Olmsted, after a good deal of backing and filling, expresses substantially the same view in the *New York Times*, Jan. 12, 1854, reprinted in *Cotton Kingdom*, 614–622.

20. *Back Country*, 279–280.

lumbering, the extraction of turpentine—and he probed into the practical aspects of plantation management as only an experienced farmer could. This led him to investigate such features as absentee ownership, the overseer system, the slave traffic, the efficiency and adaptability of the labor force, the utilization of the soil, the hiring out of slaves, the use of white workers, the range of plantation occupations other than tillage, and, in general, the question of whether the institution of servile labor paid off in dollars and cents.

He also inquired into the wider social consequences of human bondage: the effect on the masters, on the slaveless farmers, on the poor whites, on the free Negroes, and, most of all, on the chattels themselves. Were the slaves better off than black or white wage-workers in the free states? Were they better off than they would have been in Africa? What opportunities did they have for self-improvement? Was cruelty an incidental or inseparable part of the system? Did their treatment vary according to the master, the region, the size of the plantation, the nature of their work? Olmsted's scrupulousness as a witness is indicated by his avowal that in fourteen months in the South he did not himself once see a slave auction.[21] He also touches upon a side of the "peculiar institution" that posterity has generally forgotten: the fact that Negroes themselves sometimes owned slaves—a phenomenon which suggests that the system of involuntary servitude was something more than simply a convenient method of policing race relations.

On other phases of Southern life Olmsted is equally informative. He contrasts the South's stifling of the public discussion of slavery with the Northern practice of freely ventilating social abuses as a way of remedying them. If

---

21. *Seaboard Slave States*, 31 (*Cotton Kingdom*, 40–41). At another point in the *Cotton Kingdom* (14), however, Olmsted might give the unwary reader the impression that he had attended one.

slavery was as perfect a social arrangement as Southerners commonly alleged, he saw all the more reason why they should allow its merits to be debated. On the other hand, he occasionally heard private condemnations of the institution and even came across instances of familiarity with *Uncle Tom's Cabin.* Interestingly enough, he discovered one of the strongest champions of slavery in a Northern woman in Texas, herself the owner of several house servants.[22]

The meager standard of living—the shabby dwellings, the coarse and monotonous fare, the absence of cleanliness and ordinary comforts, the dearth of newspapers and other reading matter—appalled this Yankee who had never encountered anything like it in even the humblest Northern homes. From the banks of the James to the banks of the Mississippi he saw scarcely a volume of Shakespeare, a sheet of music, a good art engraving, or a reading lamp. Random conversations along the way suggested, moreover, that the level of general information was not much better. One person supposed New York was in New Orleans, another that Iowa lay somewhere west of Texas, another that New York was a slave state, while still another hadn't heard that the war with Mexico was over. Olmsted's strictures on the vaunted Southern hospitality provoked a furious rebuttal from De Bow, the New Orleans editor, only to bring from Olmsted an additional bill of particulars.[23] All these and other insights into Southern life, favorable and unfavorable, await the reader of the *Cotton Kingdom.*

22. *Journey through Texas,* 119–121 (*Cotton Kingdom,* 302–304).
23. *De Bow's Review,* XXIII (1857), 118–121. In support of his own observations Olmsted cites Godkin's similar experiences in the South in 1856–1857. *Back Country,* 61–62, 408–409 (*Cotton Kingdom,* 441–443, 551–552). He could easily have multiplied quotations from this source. See Rollo Ogden, *Life and Letters of Edwin Lawrence Godkin* (New York, 1907), I, 133, 135, 137–140, 148, 155–156. In the *New York Times,* Jan. 12, 1854, reprinted in *Cotton Kingdom,* 614–622, Olmsted, however, at one point praises Southern hospitality. Further reflection and fuller knowledge evidently caused him to alter this opinion.

II THE CITIZEN

7   *The New Tyranny*

On July 4, 1776, a band of revolutionists, sitting behind closed doors in Carpenters' Hall in Philadelphia, solemnly resolved that they could no longer endure a political yoke which had become in their eyes an intolerable tyranny, and they declared themselves to the world, a free and independent people. One hundred and fifty years later, in this year of our Lord 1926, the American people are being asked to celebrate that fateful decision, for from it has grown a mighty nation, a dynamic civilization, and a system of political principles that has enthroned the common man the world over. It seems fitting, therefore, on an occasion like this, that we should review some of the major elements which have made possible these achievements, and particularly that we should assess some of the results from the standpoint of intellectual progress.

Exactly fifty years after the adoption of the Declaration of Independence, the two men who had contributed most to its drafting lay on their deathbeds. One of them, that sturdy and irascible patriot, John Adams of Massachusetts, had served as second President of the United States, and he had

Reprinted from *The Ohio State Lantern*, Columbus, Ohio, June 15, 1926.

been succeeded in office by the other, the suave and scholarly Jefferson of Virginia. United in supporting the cause of independence, the two men had later differed as to how that independence could best be used, and had become chieftains of contending political parties. In the glare of partisan conflict their differences had seemed sharply opposed; but, reconciled in their twilight years, they perceived that they had always been striving for the same goal though along different paths. In a correspondence of extraordinary interest they reviewed the formative years of the nation and made clear that they thought well of the results. If Jefferson's letters sometimes betrayed an impatience that the people continued too much under the rule of the upper classes, the criticism was fairly countered by Adams' fear that the masses tended to acquire political power too rapidly for their own good. On the afternoon of July 4, 1826, the Golden Jubilee of independence, Adams breathed his last. His dying words were, "Jefferson still lives!" But it was not so, for the great Virginian had preceded him only a few hours before.

As these men realized, the United States of 1826 was not greatly different, except in territorial extent, from the nation which they helped to found. The freedom of the individual continued to be the chief interest of the state; public leadership belonged to the educated and the well-born; the ordinary man remained very largely a spectator of events. The United States, it might truly have been said, was a government of the people and for the people, but it had not yet become one by the people. Yet even as these venerable statesmen were breathing their last, they might have heard the distant tread of oncoming armies of plain men who were preparing to make their way into the places of power. The second half-century of independence was marked by the establishment of universal manhood suffrage and the elevation of the masses to political power. Andrew Jackson, who became President in 1829, was the first of a long series to be elected, not because they were superior to the multitude but because they were so much like them. Too naïve in their conception of democracy and unskilled in the arts of administration, this generation made many mistakes. But their errors were not irreparable, whereas the basic principles of popular government which they practiced are accepted to this day as the foundations of the American democratic structure.

Perhaps the most significant of these principles was that government must be obedient to public opinion and be constantly responsible to the people. The supreme importance of this conception cannot be challenged. It is the capstone of the democratic system of government. From its acceptance, however, flowed consequences which no well wisher of democracy can view without disquiet. If the voice of the people is the voice of God in the realm of government, why should it not be equally so in other fields of community action and decision? If the majority can override all dissent in matters of legislation, why should it tolerate differences of opinion in regard to social and moral questions?

The result of this specious reasoning was that the triumph of political democracy was attended by periodic and often prolonged outbreaks of organized lawlessness, undertaken, it was alleged, not in defiance of the constituted authorities but in order to maintain public tranquillity and the will of the community. No holder of unconventional opinions was free from muscular attention from these self-appointed and self-deceived guardians of law and order. The growth of Catholicism in the East was accompanied by mob attacks on the Irish districts of the cities and the storming of convents. The followers of another creed were hounded from Ohio to Missouri and then to Illinois, and finally were forced to flee American soil altogether. When the pioneers of the women's rights movement addressed meetings, they were greeted with jeers and insults and often with physical violence. No community seemed immune to the contagion. Boston, as well as Cincinnati, mobbed her outspoken abolitionists: Alton, Illinois, killed hers.

When de Tocqueville came to America in the 1830's, nothing so sharply challenged his attention as the spirit of intolerance which he found rampant in all fields of political and social endeavor. The visible censorship exercised by the mob seemed to him, on the whole, a less serious matter than the invisible pressure which every community exerted to make the individual conform to its approved pattern. "Public opinion," he wrote, "presses with enormous weight upon the mind of each individual; it surrounds, directs, and oppresses him." Coming from a monarchical country of Europe and counting himself a friend of democracy, he could neverthe-less declare, "I know no country in which there is so little true independence of mind and freedom of discussion as in America."

Thus, out of the very womb of triumphant democracy, in the second half-century of American independence, there was born an evil principle that robbed the individual of much of the freedom which the law intended to give him and which, along with other influences, was destined in time to erect a real tyranny of the intellect amidst the freest political institutions the world has ever known. What was more important, it threatened to deprive the community as a whole of those sources of fresh inspiration, and of those new alternatives to old ways of doing things, which form the very breath of life to a progressive society. It is a truism that the minority opinion of one generation becomes the majority opinion of the next; yet the dominant forces in society, blind to the lessons of history, were willing to sacrifice the larger interests of society to a fancied present good. That they did not wholly succeed was a testimonial to the inherent and virile individualism of the people.

As the second half-century of independence drew to a close, the thoughts of the people turned instinctively to some suitable celebration of the one hundredth anniversary of the nation's birth. Nothing seemed more appropriate than a great national exposition which should reveal the state of intellectual and material development, that the nation had attained; and, of course, no place was so fitting as the city where independence had first been proclaimed. The result was the Centennial Exposition of 1876 at Philadelphia, attended by countless thousands of Americans from all parts of the country. There the visitor, doubting the evidence of his own senses, could use a contrivance, exhibited by its inventor, a young man named Bell, for carrying on a conversation over a wire. Walking about the grounds at night, his way was lighted, brilliantly as it seemed to him, by arc lamps, invented shortly before by Brush of Cleveland. In Machinery Hall he found a bewildering display of all kinds of new and strange mechanisms which were designed to revolutionize the work of factory, farm, and mine.

THE CITIZEN

The Philadelphia Centennial was both an evidence and a promise that the nation was entering a new era—an age of machinery, of steam, steel and electricity, of scientific discovery and large-scale production. The story of this third half-century, continuing to the present year, is like a page from the Arabian Nights. No slave of the lamp performed greater miracles at the command of an Aladdin than have the Edisons, the Mergenthalers, and the Wrights during these years. Human society was transformed between the infancy and old age of an average man. The urban dweller born in an era of coal-oil lamps, horse cars, and four-story buildings died amidst the roar and rumble of a city of incandescent lighting, automobiles, and skyscrapers. The farmer toiling in his lonely fields found the good things of the city drawing nearer to him with the extension of good roads, mail-order marketing, interurban trolleys, and the telephone. In this general well-being the women of the household partook, as the drudgery of housework crumbled before the introduction of new mechanical appliances and the labor of food preparation was simplified by the efforts of the butcher, the canner, and the baker. It is not too much to say that, as a result of this unexampled advance in the physical facilities of living, the average workingman enjoys more comfort than did a medieval baron. Certain it is that if the owner of the poorest tenement house in a modern city should install the kind of plumbing that George Washington possessed, he would promptly be locked up as a menace to the health of the community.

The motive force behind these changes was machinery—machinery in its thousands of applications and countless ramifications. A new power had arisen in American life, impersonal, all-pervasive, irresistible. Originally the off-spring of the brain of man, the Machine speedily turned to the task of reshaping society according to its own needs and caprice. As if to offset its acts of beneficence, it established a dominion over man which no one had intended or foreseen. It asked for a home; and huge mills and factories were built on every hand. It demanded retainers and servitors; and millions of men, women, and children were drafted into its service. It disdained the open countryside; the great, smoky, disease-breeding cities, where men were crowded like cattle, were created for its pleasure.

Samuel Butler in his novel called *Erewhon* tells of a race of men who, alarmed at the growing power of these iron monsters and fearful lest they take on a life and conscious-ness of their own, abolished all machinery from their land. There is, I dare say, no danger that these mighty machines of ours are likely to become men; but there can be no doubt that they are causing men to become like machines. Indeed, in an age like the present when industrialism is held up as the great goal of human effort, what could be more fitting than that men should adopt machine ways of living and life itself become mechanized? The peoples of entire cities are ruled by the shrill blasts of a few factory whistles, and rise, eat, go to work, rest, toil, and sleep again at their bidding. Cities themselves have become so standardized that in traveling on a railway it is scarcely possible to distinguish one from another.

But mechanization is more than a matter of externals: it has invaded the mental and spiritual life of man as well. The newspaper reader, wherever he may be, in town or country, in East or West, sits down to the same daily diet of identically

133

worded news items, the same political cartoons and feature stories, the same advertisements, comic strips, and advice to the lovelorn. Andy Gump, and Mutt and Jeff, are the idols, not of a single community, but of the entire nation. In their hours of ease, men perforce turn for companionship to machines—to the motor car, the movie, the radio. Nor are these mechanisms mere means to an end. Take away from the automobile owner his car, and what resources of the inner life are there for him to fall back upon? The street-car conductor in the familiar story, finding himself with an unexpected vacation, spent the day riding around in a street car.

The principle of standardization, so vital for industrial efficiency, has become one of the animating principles of modern society. In imitation of the machine, an unthinking public has come to place a premium upon uniformity, homogeneity, conformity, and to abhor, except within narrow limits, diversity, differences, innovation. The incessant bombardment of standardized newspapers, magazines, books, movies, plays are causing the people not only to use the same slang, sing the same melodies, and wear the same clothes, but even to feel the same emotions and think the same thoughts. The whole force of mechanization on American culture has been toward the suppression of uniqueness, individuality, and independence in thought and conduct. The pressure exerted by society tends to make everyone cherish the aspiration of being like everyone else; and we are in danger of becoming a nation of parrots.

Thus, the Machine has taken its place alongside of Public Opinion as a contender for the mastery of the American mind. Both have found a potent ally in a distinctive attribute of the national character, which may be called the America.. genius for organization. This was a capacity of which the people had only recently become conscious. In colonial times individualistic enterprise was the dynamic principle of society, and it was only in matters of religion that the people resorted to association and cooperation. With the winning of independence, however, men devoted their organizing abilities to problems of government and politics —to the making of constitutions, the holding of conventions, and the direction of political parties. This they accomplished with such unparalleled success that the second half-century of independence saw an extension of these activities to humanitarian causes and reform movements. Thus, great national bodies were formed to agitate and promote such reforms as public education, women's rights, temperance, and antislavery.

Feeding on its own success, the spirit of organization has, during the past half-century, penetrated virtually every field of American thought and endeavor. Capital has created its great trusts and combinations; labor, its labor unions. Scholars, deserting their traditional solitude, have banded together in local and national associations. Businessmen, teachers, physicians, preachers, engineers, and undertakers, all have become involved in an intricate network of organizations with the customary elaborate paraphernalia of officers, conventions, and official publications. As the American people have acquired a greater margin of leisure from gainful labor, here too the virus of organization has done its work. It was in these years that the Americans became a nation of "joiners." Lodges and clubs sprang up on every hand, with fantastic names and secret rituals, grips, and pass-words. Nor were the women neglected. Their clubs became so numerous and widespread that more than a quarter of a century ago they, too, were able to form a national federation. Even in the realm of physical recreation, which would seem to offer a peculiar scope for individual initiative, that sport was indeed a poor one which could not show one or more national leagues and associations.

This headlong rush of persons possessing like tastes and interests to do things together is without parallel in the history of the world, and was, of course, based on the sound maxim that "in union there is strength." But what was at the outset a healthy instinct has become vitiated by overzealous practice. There is scarcely a community in the entire land that is not overorganized and in which the energy consumed in committees, clubs, and organizations is not altogether out of proportion to any good that could result. The great benefit to the individual, which should have accrued from the enjoyment of a larger measure of leisure than any people has ever before known, has been neutralized by the perpetual motion imposed by group activities. The older idea of congenial spirits shyly seeking each other for occasional communion, of individuals giving themselves of choice to periods of serious reading or reflective thinking, of husband and wife quietly sharing each other's thoughts of an evening before the fireside, has almost entirely vanished. Moreover, the notions of the club, of one's social set, of one's political party, have supplanted those standards of personal rectitude and intellectual integrity so important for the welfare both of the individual and the community. In the vital matters of self-cultivation we have abandoned the self-reliant ways of our forefathers, have forgotten the importance of privacy and repose, and have learned to hide from ourselves by seeking refuge in a crowd.

The modern tyranny, then, which confronts the American people is not that of a political despot or a military dictator. In Byron's phrase:

> Think'st thou there is no tyranny
> but that
> Of blood and chains?

Nor is it so much an oppression of the body as it is of the inner life of man. Would that it were a despotism of the usual kind, for it would then be easier for society to combat it. If my analysis is correct, it is the monstrous product of three factors in American development that in themselves should have yielded only good: Public Opinion, the Machine, and the National Genius for Organization. Grown to bloated dimensions, they have collectively imposed on the mind of man a servitude that is all the more fearful because it is impalpable and unseen, all the more powerful because it is seldom challenged.

Without a violent stretch of the imagination the typical American today may be pictured as a man wearing a Knox hat, an Arrow collar, a Manhattan shirt, a Hart, Schaffner, and Marx suit, and a pair of Walkover shoes, seated in a Ford car with a *Saturday Evening Post* under his arm on his way to the monthly meeting of the National Association for the Banishment of Privacy from the American Home. He is standardized both inside and out. Like the drapings of his body, so have the furnishings of his mind been supplied by the various agencies which operate for that purpose in modern America. The necessity for reflection and thought

137

has been eliminated from his life. In matters of religion, the church says, "Let me do your thinking for you." In matters of personal conduct, the community declares, "We will do your thinking for you." In matters of politics, the party leaders announce, "We have done your thinking for you."

In the last decade the forces making for social uniformity and the suppression of dissent have attained an unprecedented momentum. The intolerance engendered by the war helped to this end, but, after all, it did little more than intensify tendencies already well developed. One of the most flagrant manifestations of this spirit has been the rise and spread of the Ku Klux Klan. In a country bred to the Anglo-Saxon tradition of progress through law, a secret hooded order, borrowing the name of an unlawful organization of Reconstruction times, has intimidated and ruled entire communities, has waged war against racial and religious minorities, and has sought to rubberstamp its peculiar pattern of "Americanism" upon the nation.

The contagion of intolerance has ever infected legislators, who have joined in the hue and cry of those who wish to substitute a medieval obscurantism for the knowledge discovered by trained scientists and scholars. The whole nation laughed, a quarter of a century ago, when the Indiana legislature came within one reading of passing a bill for providing that the circumference of a circle should thereafter be four times the diameter instead of the vexatious 3.1416. Yet this tilt with truth was no more ridiculous than the solemn efforts that have been made in the last years by various lawmaking bodies to settle, by legislative decree, what constitutes verity in such subjects as biology and history. As Lowell wrote many years ago:

138

> Think you Truth a farthing rushlight
> to be pinched out when you will
> With your deft official fingers and
> your politicians' skill?

Yet today, in Tennessee, Florida, and North Carolina, no public school teacher can legally teach that man has descended—or even ascended—from a lower order of animal life, but must uphold (according to the Tennessee statute) "the story of the divine creation of man as taught in the Bible."

Other states, like Wisconsin and Oregon, have invaded the domain of the historical specialist, and with equal assurance have declared what manner of information regarding American history shall be imparted to public school pupils. They profess, of course, to act from motives of patriotism, but it is a frail kind of patriotism that fears lest the truth about the great men of America be unfit for young ears to hear. Moreover, in their efforts to cramp the human intellect, legislatures have had the zealous support of large organized groups of the public—a curious assortment, to be sure, but nevertheless numerous and powerful—including some of the larger Protestant denominations, the Sons and Daughters of the American Revolution, the Irish-Americans, and the German-Americans. In one cause at least, descendants of the Revolution and hyphenated Americans may labor lovingly together. It may well be asked, what has become of our vaunted belief in tolerance, of our faith in the power of truth as a force for personal and civic righteousness, of our proud boast that error is dangerous only when truth is not left free to combat it?

Thus, in this sesquicentennial year of independence, we find ourselves confronted by a strange paradox: America has achieved the greatest measure of political freedom known to history, but Americans individually have never before possessed so little intellectual and spiritual freedom. My message were indeed a counsel of despair if there were no escape from this creeping social and intellectual paralysis. One agency of society, however, has the power, the intelligence, and, I believe, the courage to break through the shackles which modern life would place upon freedom of thought and investigation. That agency is education, particularly as vitalized by the leadership of the college and the university.

But higher education itself, as we know it, is a product of the complex forces of modern life, and its character and procedure have been deeply influenced by the conditions that prevail in the outside world. Thus, there is scarcely a university in the land in which the facilities have not been sadly overtaxed by great throngs of students intent primarily on getting a technical or professional education. The emphasis of higher education has definitely shifted from the attainment of a broad liberal culture as a preparation for life to the acquisition of vocational proficiency for earning a livelihood.

Moreover, the physical difficulty of dealing with vast numbers of students has greatly complicated the problem of instruction. One hundred years ago the total college enrollment for the entire United States was 6,419; today there are almost twice that number in the Ohio State University alone. Leaders of opinion, reflecting the current subservience to industrial ideals, have been heard to speak approvingly of "educational factories" and of "mass production in education." The fact is, however, that the process of educating the human mind is not comparable to that of assembling and uniting the parts of an automobile. No principle is better established than that true education must be, in final analysis, the product of the student's own mental exertions. Yet, in our overcrowded college courses, class work, instead of allowing the freest possible scope to the development of the individual, tends to become a fixed routine. Unconsciously the main purpose of the instructor becomes to train the memory of his students rather than to stimulate their minds, to satisfy intellectual curiosity rather than to excite it, and to reward those who can best reproduce in an examination what the professor has said in class. It is not surprising that a foreign observer, after visiting some of the courses in one of our older universities, should remark, with a strong seasoning of truth, that the students acted as if they believed everything worth thinking had been thought and they were there only to gather souvenirs.

Another characteristic of the modern college is the extraordinary patchwork of courses which forms the curriculum. This curriculum was the conception of no single man nor of any single group of men. It was blown together, so to speak, by the winds of chance. As the interests of modern society have increased, one field of study after another has pushed its way into the curriculum, and the older subjects, enriched in content and point of view, have become divided into subfields with substantial bodies of knowledge of their own. Departments of instruction have multiplied, each of them zealous to secure proper representation in the general list of offerings. As President Frank recently observed, "specialization has converted our universities into intellectual department stores, or more accurately, into a series of intellectual specialty shops housed under a common roof."

The fact is that the whole system of higher education has been organized for the convenience and benefit of the teacher or specialist in a subject rather than from the point of view of the needs of the individual student. The undergraduate moves along, as in a great cafeteria, selecting dishes here and there, with no assurance that at the end he will have a balanced or digestible meal. It is little wonder that the average student thinks of education in terms of course credits, or that at the end of his fourth year he asks, "Have I sufficient credits for graduation?" rather than, "Have I mastered any considerable portion of the domain of human knowledge?" This is not the student's fault, but the faculty's; and the situation will continue until the course of study is completely reorganized with the learner's mind, rather than the teacher's, as the starting point of the educational process.

The nationwide controversy that is raging over the question of military training in the colleges illustrates again how confused our thinking has become in regard to education. The whole system of soldier training rests upon the complete subjection of one man's will to that of another. If we accept the premise that the primary reason for students going to college is to learn how to use their minds, anything which actually defeats this purpose, however desirable in itself, is to be condemned. It would seem clear, therefore, that military training, whether compulsory or voluntary, has no place in a university that is consecrated to the ideal of cultivating individual initiative, independent thinking, and intellectual leadership.

As for the modern college faculty, that institution is a rare and fortunate one in which the members of the instructional staff are not underpaid and overworked. The widely accepted myth of scholarly leisure is a snare and a delusion. It has completely broken down under the increasing weight of endless academic tasks; and the college instructor vainly envies the eight-hour day of organized labor as he strives conscientiously to execute his manifold duties as teacher, investigator, writer, director of research, committee man, student adviser, and public speaker. Once the holder of a university chair was regarded by society as a torchbearer of civilization, as an intellectual pioneer advancing the outposts of truth; now he is watched jealously for fear he may give utterance to views that run counter to the inherited opinions of the community. The professor's mind, it seems, must be standardized according to the same model as that of the public; and the unfortunate who forgets that is likely to find himself haled before some august tribunal on vague charges of "radicalism" and "bolshevism." It is a paradoxical fact that, at the same time that we are spending millions on education, we have come to fear the effects of education upon the human intellect. By some perversion of thinking we have come to regard a college as an academic hothouse where delicate minds must be shielded from the storms and controversies that rage in the world outside. Big universities can be built on this plan, but great ones never.

It is evident, therefore, that if higher education is to take a militant leadership in the struggle to save the individual, it must begin by reforming itself. If the signs of the times are to be trusted, this the authorities of our colleges are prepared to do. Fortunately man has inherited from his simian ancestors not only the capacity to ape others, but also the ability to monkey for himself. There is every reason to believe that the more progressive colleges are convinced they have gone far enough in aping one another and are now resolved to do some monkeying for themselves. Probably never before has the academic world been in so great a ferment; never before have so many significant experiments been undertaken in the effort to humanize and individualize education.

One evidence of the new trend is the development of countless junior colleges, offering only the first two years of the college course, and thus tending to relieve the great universities of congestion in their lower branches of instruction. Another is seen in the practice of endowed institutions in limiting enrollment, a policy which has usually been attended by a more careful selection of the type of students admitted. The state universities have thus far hesitated to restrict the size of their student bodies; nevertheless they, along with the private institutions, have carried on a series of novel and fruitful experiments which have as their purpose the development of the unusually gifted student, as against that of the average one. They no longer are content with the ideal of an educated mediocrity. The new doctrine is that democracy in education consists not in giving every student the same instruction but in giving to each individual mind, according to its capacity, the greatest possible incentive to growth.

There are signs too, here and there, of a willingness of college faculties to forget their departmental boundaries, and collaborate on courses which give students, in their early years, large and understanding views of great fields of knowledge. Some institutions have even gone so far as to require all students, before graduation, to take a series of general examinations covering their four years' work and involving a thorough knowledge of some one large field of study irrespective of the specific courses taken in it.

Perhaps most significant of all has been the self-assertion of the students themselves in matters relating to educational policy. They are asking, and asserting, the right to be heard on questions which, though we have often forgotten it, are more vitally related to their interests than to those of the faculty. And in an increasing number of colleges the authorities are welcoming such collaboration and finding in it a useful corrective to the present day tendency toward the mechanization of the educational process. Though this new spirit is in evidence in many places, two examples will suffice for purposes of illustration. At one institution last fall, when the students were engaged in selecting their work for the year, the undergraduate daily published a guidebook of the college courses, with candid descriptive comments which often differed radically from the accounts that appeared in the official catalogue. More recently, the Student Council of the same institution drew up a long printed report, proposing changes in the curriculum which are now under the serious consideration of the governing board. At another college last year a student committee, after visiting a number of colleges and studying their aims and methods, formulated a new curriculum which the faculty adopted.

These and numerous other signs indicate that the educational pendulum is swinging away from uniformity to

THE CITIZEN

diversity, from standardization to differentiation. The new purpose is to arm the student to do battle with those countless tyrannies of modern life which seek to destroy the individual in the mass. The new aspiration is not so much to teach young men and women how to make a living, but to help them to learn how to live a life. It was none other than Thomas Jefferson, the father of the state university system, who more than a century ago set the goal which we have yet to attain, when he declared, "I have sworn upon the altar of God eternal hostility to every form of tyranny over the human mind."

Yet the college cannot proceed far without the support of an intelligent public opinion. You who are going forth into the world will have much to do in shaping the thinking of the next generation. In the memorable words of President Coolidge uttered before the recent convention of the American Legion, "Progress depends very largely upon the encouragement of variety. Whatever tends to standardize the community, to establish fixed and rigid modes of thought, tends to fossilize society ... It is the ferment of ideas, the clash of disagreeing judgments, the privilege of the individual to develop his own thoughts and shape his own character, that makes progress possible."

Where will you stand, my friends, on this greatest of all issues? Alma Mater asks you, as educated men and women, not to exhaust your loyalty in rejoicing over her victories on the athletic field. She summons you to a greater loyalty, a higher consecration: nothing less than your undying devotion to the freedom of learning, the fearless dissemination of truth, and the emancipation of the human mind.

146

8   The True American
Way of Life

Just as Dr. Johnson said in his day that patriotism was the
last refuge of a scoundrel, so our history shows that the word
"American" has been exploited by the vicious and un-
principled. Perhaps the trouble first arose when the new-
found hemisphere was named after the wrong man—not
to commemorate its discoverer but a later and less deserving
voyager. The confusion increased when the British colonists
in North America, deciding to cast off the yoke of the mother
country, appropriated the designation Americans for themselves alone and blandly called their country the United
States of America. The Declaration of Independence, to be
sure, provided an occasion, which Jefferson magnificently
utilized, for proclaiming to the world the ideals of human
equality that animated the new nation. Though this might
have been supposed to settle the matter, the term American
in the years since then has sometimes been twisted and
tortured in ways that the founders of the Republic would
neither have recognized nor condoned.

Just to consider a few examples, the first political party
to call itself American arose in the 1850's for the purpose of
preventing Catholics and naturalized citizens from holding

Reprinted from *St. Louis Post-Dispatch*, Seventy-Fifth Anniversary Supplement, Dec. 13, 1953.

public office. The American Protective Association in the 1880's, though not a party, had a similar aim. More recently, in the 1920's, the National Association of Manufacturers sought by means of its "American Plan" to destroy national trade unions, and during the same decade the Ku Klux Klan, as self-appointed guardians of "100 percent Americanism," maimed and killed to establish "white, native, Protestant supremacy." Not to be outdone, the United States branch of the Communist party proclaimed in the 1930's that "Communism is Twentieth-Century Americanism."

Congress also got into the act, setting up the House Committee on Un-American Activities in 1938, which is still in existence and which has had counterparts in some of the states as well as currently in Congress. The House committee, hiding behind legislative immunity and infringing the constitutional guarantee of due process, displayed such reckless zeal in its accusations that in 1942 it won the commendation of the Imperial Wizard of the Ku Klux Klan. A later chairman of the committee was sent to prison for diverting government funds to his own pocket.

The time is ripe and overripe for scraping such excrescences from the meaning of Americanism and for reasserting its true import and spirit. The state of alarm and panic which has recently gripped so many citizens out of concern for preserving the American way of life seems temporarily to have sapped the qualities of courage and confidence which are ours by every right of inheritance. We have, moreover, been presenting to the world a face so lined with anxiety and fear as to daunt our friends and encourage our enemies. In our folly we have even violated some of the very liberties we profess to be safeguarding.

Clearly nothing is more important for our own sake as well as for that of the rest of mankind than to keep in mind the traits and convictions that have made the nation great and enduring in the past.

The American people are a distinctive breed. This does not mean that they are interchangeably alike. Regional, occupational, and other characteristics differentiate the individual from the mass just as in foreign lands. Nor does it mean that they do not share numerous traits with peoples elsewhere. This would be folly to deny. It means, rather, that the qualities the Americans hold in common have given them a stamp which the whole world recognizes. Far younger than any European nation, they have evolved in their shorter span of years as definite a way of life.

That way is the product of many and diverse influences. For one thing, the American has his ancestral roots in nearly every country on the globe. "All of us are descended from immigrants," as President Franklin Roosevelt felt it necessary to remind a convention of the Daughters of the American Revolution. Even the English colonists were immigrants from the standpoint of the Indian, and in the long years since then their successors arrived by the millions from all over the earth.

These newcomers were not a chosen people, but, with the sad exception of the Africans brought over in chains, they were a choosing people who deliberately quit the familiar and near to commence a new life in a strange and distant land. Yet in one sense they were also a chosen people, because only the most enterprising and self-reliant made the break. In the New World they buried their Old World feuds and learned to live together in peace and mutual helpfulness.

Members of many religious faiths, they exemplified the virtues of tolerance and demonstrated the value to society of cherishing the rights of minorities. They also contributed vitally to the material and moral development of the country as well as to the arts of civilization.

These men and their descendants found in the undeveloped continent social and economic opportunities long since foreclosed to their kinds in the homelands. Indeed, the significance of Columbus' voyage in world history lies in the chance it gave humanity to start all over again. The immigrants left behind them a rigid class structure, a state-established church, meager political privileges, and a bare subsistence. Hence they did not have to spend themselves in tearing down old and outworn institutions before building new. As Emerson well said, "We began with freedom," or, as James Russell Lowell put it, "Here, on the edge of the forest, where civilized man was brought face to face again with nature and taught to rely mainly on himself, mere manhood became a fact of prime importance." This contact with the frontier, commencing in the colonial period, was repeated with each subsequent thrust of settlement westward till the close of the nineteenth century.

The American way is deeply indebted to this historical experience. The abundance of lands and minerals not only made possible the highest standard of living any people has ever enjoyed but it gave a dignity and status to labor unknown in the Old World.

The drone had no place in the hive. Natural resources could be utilized only by resourcefulness. Moreover, the isolated settler, toiling "from daybreak to backbreak," had also be be a jack-of-all-trades, able to devise farm implements and household utensils and furniture, as well as to turn out nails, tan skins, make flour and soap. Adaptability was the price of a comfortable existence. Thus not only the gospel of work but the talent of being handy at many things became an American trait. By the same token, the husbandman developed an aptitude for mechanical invention, for every labor-saving tool ensured larger returns for the effort put in. This knack, when later turned to manufacturing and transportation, helped to produce the modern prodigies of technology. A surprising number of our nineteenth-century inventors grew up in rural surroundings.

From the earliest days, too, the pioneer was constantly on the move, hoping to better his fortunes by seeking greener pastures and nearly always succeeding. This restlessness impressed foreign observers as rootlessness. Actually, it was a vital element in converting provincial loyalties into an all-embracing allegiance to a continent-wide country. The passing of the frontier has in no wise altered the American migratory habit, though motives of pleasure now supplement the desire for economic improvement. It is not irrelevant that the American people currently own more motorcars than bathtubs, or that even today the typical citizen seldom dies in the same locality, or even the same state, in which he was born.

Given these conditions, optimism became a dominant national quality. The doctrine of progress, of the perfectibility of man, was not a pallid abstraction imported from abroad; it was native to the soil and attained the force of a moral conviction. Anybody could become somebody by merely exerting enough effort. The only class struggle the American knew or cared about was the struggle to clamber

151

out of a lower economic class into a higher one; and the sky was the limit. If this frame of mind sometimes made him an arrant braggart, it rarely tempered his zeal.

The same vein of optimism impelled Americans to reject fatalism in religion while deriving comfort and inspiration from Christ's teachings of man's intrinsic worth and human brotherhood. It caused the revolutionists of 1776 to set forth the pursuit of happiness as their inalienable right in the Declaration of Independence and led 31 states to reaffirm this conviction in their basic laws. Under the circumstances, as an observer perceived nearly a century ago, the people of the United States "are sanguine enough to believe that no evil is without a remedy, if they could only find it, and they see no good reason why they should not try to find remedies for all the evils of life."

Equality of opportunity also encouraged the American to be a rugged individualist. Having access to the bounties of nature, he wished to have as little government as possible since government, apart from enforcing law and order, could do little for him.

He nevertheless took pains to control his political institutions lest they do him harm. Rejecting the European plan of monarchy after the separation from England, the people instituted a system of self-rule and embedded in both the federal and state constitutions their right to criticize and make changes in the government and to secure their persons and property against abuses of power. As time went on, they extended the suffrage to disfranchised classes, and they even provided free tax-supported education to assist the underprivileged and promote more intelligent citizenship.

In most domains of life, however, the American preferred

to depend upon his own brain and brawn. For projects beyond his single capacity he usually joined with others in voluntary associations which were, in effect, private governments outside the government. The United States has led the world in siring such enterprises, some of them of truly mammoth proportions. They range all the way from business, professional, and labor organizations to reform groups, fraternal orders, and societies devoted to sports and other uses of leisure.

As the twentieth century approached, however, and the rise of large-scale industry plus the closing of the frontier transformed the rural nature of American society, stark individualism in the economic sphere gradually gave way to a different view of government. In truth, government had never been quite so negative as the protagonists of free enterprise asserted, for it had aided the business class with tariffs and railroad land grants, for example, as well as the Western farmers with homesteads. But now a broader conception of the welfare state émerged. Government was looked to as a positive means of preserving or restoring equality of opportunity for the common man. This attitude found political expression in such slogans as the Square Deal, the New Freedom, the New Deal, and the Fair Deal. Despite current signs in Washington to the contrary, the changed outlook promises to be a permanent feature of our way of life.

The occupation of a virgin continent facilitated the acquisition of riches and made Americans seem in foreign eyes materialists and money grubbers. But in taming the wilderness and accumulating worldly goods the pioneer was simply putting first things first, and even those who came

153

later on the scene were seldom moved by a love of gain for its own sake.

Unlike Europe, the United States has fathered few misers. The quest for wealth has been more like a game, with the winners enjoying laurels equivalent in the Old World to unearned distinctions of hereditary rank. The successful, moreover, have shared their money with others almost as freely as they made it, returning at least part of their substance to channels of social usefulness through munificent gifts and bequests. This philanthropic streak in the national character, an index of the pervasive spirit of neighborliness, appeared early and has in our own day reached fabulous dimensions. It is another of the distinguishing marks of the American way.

This generous impulse is part of a related trait: concern for the underdog. Throughout our history man's inhumanity to man has called forth reform movements to right the wrongs. These undertakings have generally been launched and financed by those in happier circumstances who, perhaps remembering the harsh lot of their ancestors in the Old World as well as their Christian duty, were resolved to fashion a kinder society. They crusaded against Negro slavery, illiteracy, poverty, intemperance, child labor, the legal subjection of wives, slum living, and many another social abuse. Here again the constitutional liberties of speech and association justified themselves, hastening the correction of injustices by making it possible to air them freely before the public.

As the physical task of subduing the continent receded into the past, the American people were able to turn to creative work in letters, scholarship, pure science, and the arts. They discovered what some of them had always perceived: that so-called useless knowledge is often the most useful for living a rich and rounded life. Now they made ample amends for their traditional indebtedness to the learning and culture of the Old World which their fathers had left. Thus at long last the affairs of the mind also became a major national trait.

In conclusion, it hardly needs to be said that the American has not consistently lived up to his heritage. He has not always been tolerant of dissent. He has not uniformly respected minority rights. He has on occasion permitted dangerous aggregations of economic power to arise. He has sometimes been indifferent to social and political wrongdoing. He has committed other sins against the democratic creed. But, in the perspective of time, such lapses have always proved temporary. The tow of history has always returned the people to their true course.

The treatment of the Negro has been the chief blot on the American way of life. It should be remembered, however, that the institution of slavery was a legacy of British rule and that the bloodiest civil war in modern times finally ended the evil. Moreover, three amendments were attached to the Constitution to confer upon the emancipated people the same rights as those of the white man, and the national conscience has never condoned denials of complete justice to the race. Nevertheless, the black man has continued to suffer from grave disabilities, and only in our own day have we seen the definite turning of the tide in his favor. Within the foreseeable future it is almost certain that he, too, will be a full beneficiary of the American way.

Above everything else, the Americans have been a nation

THE CITIZEN

unafraid. Confronted for many years with the perils and
pains of an untamed frontier, buffeted time and again by
bitter wars and depressions, they have preserved their vigor,
ingenuity, and hope, gaining new strength from each new
ordeal and showing a capacity for ever greater achievement.
Such a people need not fear for the future. They have only
to build on the solid accomplishments of their past.

9 War and Peace in American History

"This war will not end with the duration," a Hibernian friend told Mrs. Kate O'Hare McCormick. Of this fact recent discussions give ample evidence. As the offensive strength of the United Nations has increased, so also has interest in the nature of the peace. In America particularly, insistent demands have arisen from both official and unofficial quarters for some form of international organization which will ensure the right of men to live undisturbed by fear or want or under institutions of their own choosing. Some of these utterances are pitched on the lofty plane of what Jefferson once called the "unalienable rights" of mankind. Others point to the intolerable situation presented by a shrinking earth constantly exposed to brutish subjection by a demonic power hurling thunderbolts from the sky. Still others base their appeal on the seamless web of the world's economic life, which renders every nation an inseparable part of the whole. These discussions, unhappily, ring with hollow echoes of similar discussions in the years 1915–1918. As then, popular sentiment rallies strongly, even desperately, to the thought of making this a war to end war. As then, also, the former isolationists and appeasers in public life discreetly hold their tongues while the threat to national

Reprinted from *New Republic*, CVII (Sept. 21, 1942).

survival endures or, if facing an election, seek refuge in a fog of words. One is reminded of the devil who, when sick, the devil a monk would be, but who, when well, the devil a monk was he.

One strength of the isolationists' argument on the earlier occasion was their appeal to American tradition; and therefore it seems desirable, apart from all other considerations currently urged for our cooperation in a world structure for peace, to understand what bearing American history really has on the matter. History should be an important ally of statecraft, for its function is greatly to enlarge the range of our experience by letting us see how our forerunners met similar difficulties. It permits us to base our judgments upon a vertical as well as a horizontal view of events. But history must be rightly understood to serve as a safe guide, and by the same token its teaching must not be distorted for personal or political advantage.

The foes of the League reared their historical argument upon Washington's counsel in his Farewell Address against entangling alliances. For reasons not difficult to fathom, they did not consider equally immutable—in fact, they utterly disregarded—his stern warning in the same document against "the baneful effects of the spirit of party," though it is evident that, according to the lights of 1796, he deemed the one as serious an evil as the other. The basic fallacy, of course, lay in attributing to Washington a clairvoyance that foresaw all the world developments of the next hundred years and more. Henry Cabot Lodge, biographer of the first President, put the matter judiciously in a public address in 1916: "I do not believe that when Washington warned us against entangling alliances he meant for one moment that we should not join with other civilized nations of the world if a method could be found to diminish war and encourage peace." Only later, when he became involved in the bitter fight over "Mr. Wilson's League," did he conclude that Washington, after all, meant literally what he said.

If the devil can cite Scripture for his purpose, the politician has even less trouble in bending history to his uses. In both cases the method is the same: to omit everything that contradicts the predetermined thesis, to exalt the particular over the general, to stress the letter rather than the spirit. But the usableness of the past consists not in choosing from among a welter of inconsistent tendencies, but in ascertaining the underlying direction of events. What were the conditioning influences, the persistent problems, the characteristic reactions of the public? From this point of view three deductions from our past behavior have an urgent relevance to the present situation.

In the first place, the record shows that the American people have never been able to keep out of any foreign war involving naval operations in the Atlantic. Isolationism has worked only in the periods between Europe's great wars when, of course, there was no need for it. In our colonial infancy we were drawn into the mother country's recurrent contests with France for global supremacy. Between 1689 and 1763 we took part in King William's War, Queen Anne's War, King George's War, and the French and Indian War. These were the American counterparts of the War of the League of Augsburg, the War of the Spanish Succession, the War of the Austrian Succession, and the Seven Years' War. Though Thomas Paine and other patriots argued that freedom from Great Britain would bring freedom from the power politics of the Old World, the very struggle for colonial independence eventuated in a fifth world melee. England's defeat at Saratoga in October 1777 nerved France and Spain to attack her, and presently the Netherlands joined in the assault, with a group of other maritime powers assuming hostile array as the Armed Neutrality League.

Nor did the actual achievement of independence afford the expected immunity, for the French Revolution and the rise of Napoleon soon opened a new chapter in the ancient rivalry of France and Britain. Despite every conceivable effort to remain aloof, the United States, whose commerce was exposed to constant depredation by both sets of belligerents, became embroiled in a naval war with France in 1798, which lasted for over two years, and in 1812 plunged into a second and longer war with England. For the next hundred years Europe's game of power politics left the Atlantic undisturbed, and Britannia, constantly growing toward greater democracy at home, ruled the waves without prejudice to our national interests. Not till 1914 did a situation recur which brought again into play the forces that revealed the essential identity of American safety with the control of the Atlantic by a friendly power. Germany's submarine campaign against British sea power, with its prospect of eventual success, undermined this indispensable condition of our peaceable national existence, and in 1917 we once more unsheathed the sword.

President Roosevelt has asked for an appropriate name for the present struggle. There is only one that encompasses all the facts: the Ninth World War. Viewed in the perspective of American history, the principal difference between the current contest and the earlier ones is that our national security is now threatened on the Pacific as well as the Atlantic. As long as we continue to regard these recurrent involvements as separate and unrelated events, just so long will we be content to deal with them by means of temporary expedients. But when the American public comes fully to realize that this is the same old war being fought over again for the ninth time in two hundred and fifty years, we may expect an uprising of the human spirit which will oblige statesmen to address themselves to the task of finding a genuine cure.

The second generalization that emerges from sifting the past is that the nation has never been ready militarily for any war it has ever undertaken. As someone has observed, we are a bellicose but unmilitary people. The habit of unpreparedness is not rooted in a particularly pacific history. Even during the century of peace on the Atlantic, the United States fought the Mexican War, the Civil War, and the Spanish War. The explanation lies, rather, in our preference for individualistic methods of warfare, a plan which worked well not only on the frontier but also against the British regulars at Concord and Lexington. This traditional attitude derived further warrant from a sense of security erroneously presumed to be afforded by geographic removal from the trouble-breeding centers of the Old World. Another factor was the essential humaneness of the American people who, though willing to fight, were unwilling to regard fighting as a permanent profession. From early times, also, men feared a military establishment as a menace to both peace and democracy.

Whatever the historical reasons, the consequence has been

that in every major war we have had to begin by losing it before we could begin to win it. Our struggle for independence would probably have failed but for the help in men, ships, and munitions provided by France when she entered the fray. In the War of 1812 we were so slow in bringing our strength to bear that the enemy was able to ravage the national capital; and our one smashing success, Jackson's triumph at New Orleans, came after the conclusion of peace, too late to gain the objects for which we had taken up arms. Similarly in the Civil War the tide of battle ran against the Union for the first two years, constantly exposing Washington to capture by the Confederates. In 1917 the nation was as poorly prepared. According to Brigadier General John M. Palmer, U.S.A. (retired), writing nearly a quarter of a century later, "Our capacity for military intervention in Europe was negligible. In fact, we were not even organized to defend our own shores." It took a full year to place a substantial body of troops on the European battlefront and they had to fight with machine guns, heavy artillery, and aircraft supplied largely by the British and French. Our recent record of disaster in the Far East is the latest reminder of our chronic state of unpreparedness.

Must we go on forever in the future snatching victory from defeat in this most costly of all ways? Yet is it probable that a people stubbornly indifferent to the national defenses throughout its past will be willing to convert itself permanently into an armed camp? Wisdom would seem to require an alternative way of assuring national safety without the necessity of a huge military establishment.

The third inference from American history relates to the making of peace rather than of war. Just as we have never planned properly for war, so also we have seldom planned properly for peace. Too often the horrors of the one have been followed by the horrors of the other. Though the protracted struggle for independence bound the colonists by ties of common self-sacrifice, the cessation of hostilities plunged the country into eight long years of unrest, strife, and governmental frustration. This "Critical Period," as John Fiske called it, came to an end only with the adoption of the Constitution. The peace treaty with Mexico in 1848 greatly intensified sectional divisions in American politics by failing to settle the question of Negro slavery in the new acquisitions. An armed struggle might have ensued but for the Compromise of 1850. In a similar fashion the Civil War was succeeded by the agonizing problems of Southern Reconstruction. While the war was still being waged, President Lincoln had put forward his own humane terms of reunion; but the reception of the proposal by his own party chieftains gives little reason to believe that, even if he had escaped the assassin's bullet, he could have imposed his views on Congress.

In the First World War with Germany President Wilson grasped time by the forelock and began formulating peace conditions before America became a party to the conflict. As early as December 1916 he outlined to the British government his ideas of a just settlement and offered to call a peace conference at which he would act as mediator. In January 1917 he addressed the Senate on the subject, indicating the terms acceptable to the United States. After our intervention in the struggle he elaborated these views in the famous Fourteen Points. The Allies at the peace table ignored many of his demands, but they conceded his most cherished object, the League of Nations. Through this means Wilson hoped to repair the mistakes and injustices of the treaty as well as to ensure future world peace. But it was this feature of the treaty more than any other that caused it to be rejected by the Senate.

Few people today remember, however, that a substantial majority of the Senators favored ratification. When the crucial balloting occurred on March 19, 1920, a switch of seven negative votes would have produced the requisite two-thirds majority. By so narrow a margin did the United States miss entering the League. It is true that the resolution of ratification included the Lodge reservations, but these differed only in phraseology from the Hitchcock reservations which Wilson was willing to accept. The historical student will agree with Senator William Borah's opinion five years after the event: "If we had gone into the League with the Lodge reservations, that would have been the last that there would ever have been heard of the Lodge reservations."

Had Wilson not suffered a physical breakdown at a critical point in the treaty fight, or had he been able to appeal to the country by the modern means of the radio, he would probably have succeeded in forcing through ratification on his own terms. Thirty-two legislatures had gone on record for the League. A *Literary Digest* poll early in the contest indicated an overwhelming backing by newspaper editors, most of them unconditionally. As late as two months after the Senate vote, Lodge wrote privately on the eve of the Republican convention, "I think the bulk of the convention and the mass of the people at the present moment are in favor of the treaty with the reservations which bear my name."

Unhappily, the issue was never squarely submitted to the

electorate. Though Wilson asked that the election of 1920 take "the form of a great and solemn referendum," the Republicans ran Senator Harding, a Lodge reservationist, on a platform that faced all directions at once. The isolationists insisted it meant rejection of the League, while a group of thirty-one distinguished Republicans, including Elihu Root, Herbert Hoover, and Charles E. Hughes, instructed the voters that the question before them was "not between a league and no league," but whether the one offered by President Wilson should be accepted unchanged or changed. Only after his overwhelming victory did Harding discover that the outcome meant that the League "is now deceased."

If the United States had united with the forty-two (later sixty) other nations, as a majority of the people clearly wished, the whole history of the postwar period might have been different. America was the only Great Power in a position to view Old World controversies impartially. Her influence both psychologically and materially would have been a constant makeweight for settling international disputes peaceably before they reached grave proportions. Remaining aloof, we not only deprived the League of this advantage, but we also jeopardized the success of its principal coercive weapon: the application of economic sanctions. The United States was the greatest trading nation in the world; and since it could not be counted upon to join in economic sanctions against aggressor powers, the League was reduced to a policy of timidity and talk. Japan, Italy, and Germany in turn defied the League and, having demonstrated its impotence, combined in a scheme to partition the earth.

What conclusions shall we draw from these persistent factors in our history? No thinking American can entertain a moment's doubt. However hardheaded he may be, however unresponsive to idealistic impulses, however governed by purely selfish considerations, he cannot fail to find in the plain facts of the case a call to present action. Since it is our fate to be inevitably embroiled in Europe's recurrent struggles, we must place ourselves in a position to help cure injustices before they foment the war spirit. Since it is contrary to our national temperament to be always armed to the teeth, common sense dictates that we should join other peace-loving peoples in a collective system strong enough to hold aggressor powers in curb. And since we have hitherto neglected to use war as a constructive instrument for peace, we must try as never before to ensure that the present conflict has a different outcome.

The events of the past few years suggest that we are tardily determined to correct these ancient errors. As early as 1937 President Roosevelt in his "quarantine" speech began to use the influence of his office to try to check the drift toward war. At the time of the Czecho-Slovakian crisis in 1938 he informed Germany: "I am persuaded that there is no problem so difficult or so pressing for solution that it cannot be justly solved by the resort to reason rather than by the resort to force." To all he made clear the principle upon which he acted: "When peace is broken anywhere it is threatened everywhere." When Europe in spite of his efforts plunged once more into the abyss, he embarked upon a program of extending aid to the Allies "short of war." Through a series of measures climaxed by the lend-lease act he turned the United States into the "arsenal of democracy." It was a daring and unprecedented course, but it afforded the best hope of an Allied victory before history repeated itself and we ourselves should be sucked into the maelstrom. At the same time the President tried to make up for earlier neglect by strengthening the national defenses. At his behest Congress began the construction of a two-ocean navy, enlarged the regular army, and adopted the first peacetime conscription in our history. By executive decree he acquired the eight naval bases from Britain as ramparts against possible Axis attack and he concluded defense arrangements with Canada and the Latin American republics.

Finally, like President Wilson, he took steps while still a neutral to attempt to shape the peace settlement; but improving upon Wilson's method, he obtained advance agreement from the powers fighting the enemy. Meeting in mid-ocean in August 1941, President Roosevelt and Prime Minister Churchill drew up the so-called Atlantic Charter enunciating the principles on which they "base their hopes for a better future for the world." These affirmations include the right of every people to choose its own form of government, the fullest collaboration among nations for facilitating trade and improving standards of living, the right of all peoples to dwell in safety within their own borders, and, finally, the disarming of the aggressor powers "pending the establishment of a wider and permanent system of general security." Within six weeks the Soviet Union and the free governments of nine other countries subscribed to these tenets, and shortly after Pearl Harbor the twenty-six United Nations declared the Atlantic Charter "a common program of purposes and principles." Within two weeks more the twenty-one republics of the Western Hemisphere took a similar stand. In all, thirty-eight different governments gave their adherence before the end of January 1942. To clinch the economic objectives, the State Department further inserted in all the master lend-lease agreements a mutual pledge (open to participation by all other countries) to promote "the betterment of worldwide economic relations" in the postwar period.

The peacemakers at the close of this war, unlike their predecessors of 1919, will find it difficult to disown these constructive aims. President Roosevelt's mistake may lie, rather, in his failure to commit Congress or the Senate to the "common program of purposes and principles." As in Wilson's day, men obsessed with an escapist psychology in international affairs may clamor to keep America from joining a "permanent system of general security" and from pursuing a liberal policy in world economic relations. Again they may make the welkin ring with the delusive virtues of isolationism, of an America sheltered from aggression by geographic remoteness, of a hermit nation able to live apart from the rest of mankind. Should that come to pass, there is comfort in the thought that the voters are not so likely to let themselves be duped as they were the last time. From the vantage point of two hundred and fifty years of American experience they may be expected to learn from the errors of the past and to resolve at long last to put history to work for the national good. And no lesson of history stands out more baldly than that collective security is the best safeguard of American security.

10 Do We Have National Unity?

The bombing of Pearl Harbor hushed the voices of discord in America with a suddenness that has excited suspicion in some quarters as to the genuineness of the conversion. Is the new-found national unity firmly based? Will it stand the gaff of discouraging delays, repeated military reverses, and cunning defeatist propaganda? In an affirmative answer lies not only the effectiveness of our all-out effort but also the best assurance of a durable peace. But is an affirmative answer warranted?

There are various ways of gauging national unity. It may be regarded as a philosophical concept or, if you will, reduced to a mathematical formula. No responsible statesman in any country, however, would be willing to base his course on an abstraction. He knows, as every student of history knows, that national unity is a relative matter— relative to the people concerned, the nature and extent of the crisis, and the unity or disunity of the enemy nation. In totalitarian countries the problem is obviously simpler than in democratic ones. And in democratic countries no better clue to the present can be found than in the way the people have behaved on similar occasions in the past.

Reprinted from *New Republic*, CVI (Feb. 2, 1942).

America engaged in four major wars prior to the twentieth century; and according to any ideal standard, the lack of national unity was, in every instance, shocking. John Adams reckoned that a third of the colonists—about 800,000 out of approximately 2,400,000—opposed the Revolution; and a fellow patriot, Thomas McKean of Philadelphia, while not disagreeing, was of the opinion that "more than a third of influential characters were against it." "New York and Pennsylvania," wrote Adams, "were so nearly divided, if their propensity was not against us, that if New England on one side and Virginia on the other had not kept them in awe, they would have joined the British." To quench this fire in the rear the patriots resorted to intimidation and violence, while the more prominent Tories were exiled and their lands and property expropriated. It is estimated that a hundred thousand fled the scene. Parliament eventually compensated them to the amount of £3,292,500.

Three decades later, when the sword was unsheathed for a second time against Britain, the fissures in public opinion proved equally deep. Again John Adams believed that a third of the people disapproved of the war, though he himself favored it. The peace sentiment centered in the minority party, the Federalists, who represented the Northern commercial and shipping interests eager to continue trading connections with England. When war was declared, the Federalist members of the House of Representatives adopted an address stigmatizing the conflict as "a party and not a national war" entered upon by "a divided people." The governors of Connecticut and Massachusetts declined to allow their militia to be put into the field under federal command, and the people of northern New England carried on an extensive trade with the enemy across the Canadian boundary. By the close of 1813 all the New England governors were Federalists and appeasers. The Massachusetts Senate, condemning the war as "waged without justifiable cause," pronounced against any legislative "approbation of military or naval exploits which are not immediately connected with the defense of our seacoast and soil."

In October 1814, when American morale was dashed by the burning of Washington, the New England disaffection reached its climax in the calling of the famous Hartford Convention. Meeting in December, the more conservative delegates managed to hold the rasher spirits in check. Instead of the anticipated declaration for secession, the convention resolved: "A severance of the Union by one or more states against the will of the rest, and especially in time of war, can only be justified by absolute necessity." At the same time, however, the assemblage insisted on certain amendments of the Constitution, one of which would have required a two-thirds majority of both houses of Congress for declaring war or engaging in other acts of hostility. A second convention was to be held in case these demands should not be met. This menacing movement, however, quickly stumbled into its grave with the news of Jackson's victory at New Orleans and the conclusion of peace.

The Mexican War rent the nation once more with internal dissension. James K. Polk, elected President by the Democrats in 1844, precipitated the war by dispatching troops to take over a strip of territory claimed by Mexico and, when the Mexicans resisted, blamed them for initiating the conflict. "War exists," he told Congress on May 11, 1846, "and, notwithstanding all our efforts to avoid it, exists by the act of

Mexico herself." At once a storm of anger blew up from the Whig press. In torrid language the opposition denounced the war as "treason against God" instigated by Southern politicians for more slave territory. A convention of New England workingmen resolved that "we will not take up arms to sustain the Southern slaveholder in robbing one-fifth of our countrymen of labor." James Russell Lowell launched a caustic satirical attack in "The Biglow Papers." In his annual message of December 1846, Polk bitterly commented on the lack of national unity: "The war has been represented as unjust and unnecessary, and as one of aggression on our part on a weak and injured enemy . . . A more effectual means could not have been devised to encourage the enemy and protract the war."

But the worst was yet to come. In 1846–47 the legislatures of Vermont, Rhode Island, Massachusetts, and Maryland condemned the administration's purposes. The Bay State lawmakers called on "all good citizens to join in efforts to arrest this war." Northern newspapers demanded that Congress stop the bloodshed by withholding supplies. The Whig members, though unwilling to go so far, kept up an increasing barrage of criticism in which both Abraham Lincoln of Illinois and Alexander H. Stephens, later Vice President of the Confederacy, took part. In January 1848, the House of Representatives formally resolved, by a vote of 85 to 81, that the war had been "unnecessarily and unconstitutionally begun by the President of the United States." A month later the peace movement abruptly ended when vanquished Mexico signed the Treaty of Guadalupe Hidalgo.

The next war saw the American people themselves engaged in desperate combat with one another. In this struggle to preserve the Union the North might have been expected to present an undivided front, but such was not the case. As the Southern states began to secede after Lincoln's election in 1860, leaders of Northern opinion counseled a do-nothing policy. The *New York Tribune*, most influential of the nation's newspapers, declared: "If the cotton states shall become satisfied that they can do better out of the Union than in it, we insist on letting them go in peace." A national convention of workingmen at Philadelphia agreed that "Our government never can be sustained by bloodshed but must live in the affections of the people." Other groups, though for different reasons, took a similar stand. Abolitionists like William Lloyd Garrison and Senator Charles Sumner welcomed secession as a means of cleansing the North of any responsibility for slavery, while businessmen, anxious about the collection of $300,000,000 worth of Southern debts, also favored peaceful dissolution. Mayor Fernando Wood even proposed that New York constitute herself a free city and continue trade with both sections.

Like the Japanese assault on Pearl Harbor, the firing on Fort Sumter in April 1861 placed all these elements of public opinion, including for a time Wood himself, squarely behind Lincoln's policy of coercion. There remained, however, a powerful pro-Southern sentiment in the North, notably among the Democrats of the Ohio Valley states where many of the inhabitants were of Southern stock. As the war progressed, these irreconcilables, popularly known as Copperheads, carried on an appeasement propaganda in the press and on the stump, and many of them banded together in secret oath-bound societies under such names as the Knights of the Golden Circle, the American Knights, and the Sons of Liberty. These organizations harbored military as well as political designs, and Clement L. Vallandigham, their Supreme Commander in 1864, claimed an active membership of half a million—a figure accepted by the Judge Advocate General of the United States as approximately correct.

The Copperheads wielded their greatest influence in 1863, the most critical year of the war. In Indiana they prevented the legislature from adopting any measure in support of the war, while in Lincoln's own state of Illinois the House of Representatives declared for an immediate armistice and a negotiated peace. In Ohio the contest centered about the stormy figure of ex-Congressman Vallandigham. Arrested for declaring in a public speech that the war was "wicked and cruel" and waged "for the purpose of crushing out liberty and erecting a despotism," he was condemned by a military tribunal to imprisonment for the duration of the war. President Lincoln, who had had no advance knowledge of the event, shrewdly commuted the sentence to banishment to the Confederacy. While Vallandigham was still on Southern soil, he was nominated for governor by the Ohio Democrats; and escaping through the federal blockade, he conducted an active campaign from across the border in Canada. Though defeated in the election, he received 187,000 votes, 40 percent of the whole. He might have won the governorship but for two events: 39,000 out of the 41,000 soldier votes from the field were cast against him; and the flagging spirits of the civilian population were revived by the federal successes at Vicksburg and Gettysburg.

Even as late as the presidential election of the next year the Copperheads continued active, though with diminishing effect. Toward the end of the summer Lincoln privately recorded the opinion that it seemed "exceedingly probable that this administration will not be reëlected." The Democratic platform, drafted under Copperhead influence, called the war "four years of failure" and demanded immediate peace negotiations to restore the Union. In accepting the nomination, however, General George B. McClellan, the victor of Antietam, repudiated these sentiments and left the country uncertain as to what course a Democratic administration would pursue. Nevertheless, Republican success remained doubtful until the great victories won by Sherman, Sheridan, and Farragut in September definitely turned the tide. Even then, Lincoln gained reelection by only 55 percent of the popular vote, the Southern states of course not participating. Five months later the Confederacy collapsed.

If modern warfare could be carried on with the degree of national disunity that prevailed on these past occasions, no citizen need suffer a sleepless hour today. But the lessons of history are not always what they seem. Two conditions obtained in these earlier wars which have been strikingly absent from our twentieth-century conflicts. First, American disunity was matched by similar disunity in the enemy countries. At least, this was true in every case but the War of 1812, and in that war, it will be remembered, America signed a peace treaty without gaining any of the points for which she had taken up arms. In the second place, success in the field rested on the exertions of an armed fraction of the population, not on a unified effort of the nation as a whole. In both these respects the First and Second World Wars lie in a different category. In each instance America has been confronted by a consolidated militaristic state in which internal dissent was ruthlessly suppressed, and she has also been confronted, though with differences in degree, by the necessity of mobilizing her total manpower, civilian and military.

Because of these considerations President Wilson and President Roosevelt faced a new and unprecedented problem of national unity. For reasons which can only be lightly touched on here, Wilson's difficulties were the greater. The public, long indifferent to the twists and turns of European power politics, was stunned by the outbreak of a war which even most of our historians had not foreseen. Old-fashioned American isolationists joined hands with the millions of citizens of German and Austrian birth in a ceaseless campaign to keep the United States from becoming involved; and the numerous Irish element lent their support out of hatred of England. Wilson himself did little to clarify the people's thinking. Not only did he ask them at the start to be "impartial in thought as well as in action," but as late as January 1917 he expressed the hope that the war might end in a "peace without victory." When at last he decided on intervention, he had suddenly to convert a substantial section of public opinion to his own eleventh-hour convictions. This he did with incomparable eloquence and an appeal to fundamental American ideals which no statesman of today has equaled. And the people responded wholeheartedly, as to the exhortations of a great evangelist. Apart from a faction of the Socialists, no organized group remained to oppose the war.

The background of the present war presents a wholly different story. The American public, far from being ignorant of European affairs, has for many years had an almost continuous education in them. Ever since the peace of 1919 the outside world has, in one way or other, insistently intruded on our national privacy; and since 1933 Germany has perpetrated greater indecencies than the most feverish American imaginations of 1917–18 had conceived possible. Moreover, distant events have been made vivid for us by the movies and have been brought into our very homes by the radio, while the arrival of German and Italian refugees in many communities added the compelling element of intimate personal drama.

Nor have Americans of foreign stock been so ready as before to support an isolationist policy. Since the application of the national-origins regulation of 1929, the incoming stream has been reduced to a trickle, and the children and grandchildren of the older immigrants from Germany and Italy have had fewer bonds of sentiment with their home-lands. Even the Irish-American hatred of England has somewhat cooled since the setting up of the Free State in 1922. Finally, where President Wilson groped in the dark, President Roosevelt began arousing the American people to the dangers of totalitarianism long before the war of 1939 began. As far back as October 1937 he called for a combined effort of peace-loving nations to "quarantine" the aggressor powers, and on every possible occasion he returned to the theme of the irrepressible conflict between the two ways of life.

In November 1914, three and a half months after the First World War began, the *Literary Digest* discovered that, out of 367 newspaper editors polled, 242 were neutral in sympathy, 105 favored the Allies and 20 Germany. By contrast, a Gallup poll in February 1939, seven months before the Second World War broke out, indicated that 69 percent of the population favored Britain and France to the point of supporting them by every means "short of war."

As the crisis grew and Europe went to war, the dust raised by the Wheelberghs tended to conceal the ground swell of American opinion, but the actions taken by Congress spoke loudly to those willing to hear. In the period of neutrality from 1914 to 1917 the Wilson administration, despite repeated submarine sinkings by the Germans and the supposed influence of Wall Street and munitions makers, adopted no measures "short of war" for thirty months, when the merchant ships were first armed. The Roosevelt leadership repealed the arms embargo within two months of the beginning of the war (a step unnecessary in Wilson's time), adopted universal conscription within twelve months (a measure not even proposed by Wilson until after America's entry), effected the destroyer-naval base deal within the same span of time, began financing Britain's war effort under lend-lease within eighteen months, and, after establishing a naval patrol for convoy purposes, authorized the arming of merchantmen within twenty-six months. And in the case of most of these measures public opinion, as indicated by the Gallup polls, was ahead of the Congress. To be sure, Wilson's Congress took only four months longer to declare war than did Roosevelt's; but on one point at least the Wheelberghs were right: we entered this war a long time before we declared it.

When President Roosevelt told Congress in his address on January 6: "The Union was never more closely knit together and this country was never more deeply determined to face the solemn tasks before it," history amply warranted the assertion. As the record shows, never before has national unity approached so close to national unanimity. The people are sustained by a conviction gradually formed as a result of the iron logic of events, and patiently interpreted and directed by the President in a way which assures him a place among our greatest chief executives. Compared with earlier times, even 1917, there is less revivalistic fervor in the popular attitude. Instead of the hurrah spirit there is a mood of quiet, grim resolution, a determination to see the ugly business through to the finish at whatever cost.

National unity of this new kind bodes well for the years after the peace. We have the best chance we have ever had to escape the usual postwar letdown, the usual revulsion of feeling, the usual backsliding after sudden conversion. It seems highly unlikely that our people will lightly cast off heavy responsibilities so soberly undertaken. In this prospect lies the best hope for a new and effective international structure for peace, a United Nations of the World.

11   Extremism in American Politics

The presidential campaign of 1964 introduced the word "extremism" into our political vocabulary as a synonym for ultraconservatism, but the phenomenon itself is anything but new. Throughout our history it has lurked under the surface of public life, finding an escape hatch at more or less definite intervals. Psychologically the outbreaks have also borne striking resemblances, even though the professed objectives have shifted as occasion required. For these reasons a consideration of the leading examples should contribute to a better understanding of this recurring aspect of American politics.

Nearly a century and a half ago, in 1826, the abduction and presumed murder of one William Morgan of Batavia in western New York set off a wave of popular hysteria that became a force in state and national affairs. Morgan, a bricklayer, was a Mason who had written a book exposing the order's secrets, and widespread report instantly attributed his disappearance to retaliation on the part of vengeful members. When four persons were found guilty just of the kidnaping and got off with light sentences, suspicion of the

Reprinted from *Saturday Review*, Nov. 27, 1965, pp. 21–25.

fraternity's covert control of the courts, and probably also of all other departments of the government, hardened into certainty. Incidentally, the most diligent search failed to yield any trace of "the martyr's" body. The mystery remains to this day.

From New York the excitement spread to New England and the Middle Atlantic states as well as inland to Ohio and Indiana. Antimasonic newspapers and magazines sprang up to fan the flames. Traveling lecturers denounced the "hydra-headed monster." Churches expelled Masonic preachers and laymen. Many lodges disbanded; in New York state alone their number dropped from six hundred in 1826 to fifty in 1834. The Antimasons successfully ran candidates in local and state elections; several legislatures banned extra-judicial oaths; and Rhode Island and Pennsylvania required all secret societies henceforth to reveal their proceedings in annual reports.

In the national arena, politicians like Thurlow Weed and William H. Seward in New York and Thaddeus Stevens in Pennsylvania, seeking to oust President Jackson and the Democratic party from power in 1832, seized on the furor to consolidate a nationwide opposition. In doing so, however, they injected other issues and wrenched the movement so far from its original purpose that William Wirt, the Anti-masonic nominee, failed to condemn the order in his letter of acceptance. Though both Jackson and Henry Clay, the National Republican candidate, were active or former Masons, Wirt received only Vermont's seven electoral votes, while his rivals won 219 and 49 respectively.

The party then soon flickered out. The reason, according to a committee of the Pennsylvania legislature, was that "it envies the possessors of office. It is ignorant. It absurdly denounces as a mysterious institution full of guilt and blood a society of which . . . ten or fifteen thousand of our most useful, intelligent, and eminent citizens of all parties are members." Probably more decisive was the fact that questions of crucial national importance such as the tariff and the United States Bank had arisen to give the voters something more tangible to worry about.

Already events were setting the stage for a new exhibition of frenzy. Oddly enough, these alarmists saw no danger in mystic brotherhoods and in due course donned the cloak of secrecy themselves. Their fear arose from the large inflow of Irish and Germans into the United States in the 1830's and 1840's, with the Irish in particular arousing wide hostility. As Catholics they seemed to menace America's traditional Protestantism, and as a copious supply of cheap labor they jeopardized the living standards of native workers. Rumors also coursed far and fast of "Romish" plots to subvert the public schools and even the republic itself.

The popular reaction was swift and tempestuous. In 1834 a mob burned down a convent school in Charlestown, Massachusetts, and later years saw rioting, often attended with bloodshed as well as incendiarism, in New York, Philadelphia, Detroit, Louisville, and elsewhere. Anti-Catholic lecturers and periodicals flourished. In 1836 a pretended ex-nun, Maria Monk, published her *Awful Disclosures* of imagined immorality and infanticide in a convent, which sold 300,000 copies before the Civil War. Even Samuel F. B. Morse, the portraitist and inventor of the telegraph, took up arms against Rome with his *Foreign Con-*

spiracy against the Liberties of the United States (1834) and later tracts.

In the ensuing decade the nativists formed secret fraternal organizations to further the cause, such as the Order of United Americans, the Junior Order of United American Mechanics, and the Order of the Star-Spangled Banner. The last band, established in 1849 and the most militant of the lot, in turn set afoot the American or Know-Nothing party. The Know Nothings, popularly so dubbed because they denied to inquirers knowledge of the party's existence, demanded the exclusion of all foreign-born from office ("Americans must rule America"), a twenty-one-year naturalization period for voting, and the rigid separation of church and state. Aided by the nationwide consternation over the revival of the slavery controversy by the Kansas-Nebraska Act in 1854, and conducting no public campaign, they carried Massachusetts, Pennsylvania, and Delaware in the fall elections, also sent seventy-some supporters to Congress, and a year later captured five more states.

Exhilarated by these successes, the Know Nothings in 1856 nominated a national standard-bearer, the Whig ex-President Millard Fillmore, thereby bringing the historic Whig party to an end. By now, however, feeling throughout the country had reached such a pitch over the sectional question that the Know Nothings themselves could no longer ignore it, and it opened serious rifts in their convention. Although Fillmore mustered nearly a quarter of all the popular votes, they were so scattered as to win only Maryland's eight electoral ones. Another fledgling party, the Republican, founded expressly to curb the expansion of slavery, obtained a much larger popular support and the 114 electroral votes of eleven states. Though it, too, lost to the Democrats, it could look confidently to the future. The Know Nothings shortly passed into oblivion.

How potent a force they might have become had the sectional issue not intruded no one can say. Yet, as the Antimasonic movement showed and later evidence confirmed, such conflagrations in America have always quickly burned themselves out. While the Know-Nothing convulsion was still at its height, the politically observant Horace Greeley declared it would "vanish as suddenly as it appeared." And the Indiana Congressman George W. Julian, writing after the fact, undoubtedly expressed the sober second thought of the electorate in terming it "a horrid conspiracy against decency, the rights of man, and the principle of human brotherhood."

The next great outbreak of fear and hate occurred after the Civil War, this time in the conquered South. The remaking of race relations by Congress in the measures known as Reconstruction had distorted the section's traditional pattern of life beyond recognition. The slaves were now not only free but were voters and officeholders helping run the reconstituted state governments to the exclusion of the old master class. For ingrained believers in white supremacy this reversed the natural order of things and meant the region's "Africanization."

With no relief to be expected from a Northern-controlled Congress or at the polls, the aroused whites formed clandestine societies of resistance. The Ku Klux Klan, the best known, started in 1866 at the little town of Pulaski in southern Tennessee as a social club of returned Confederate veterans who for fun rode about the countryside after dark, masked and clad in white on white-sheeted horses. But when the weird proceedings were seen to excite the superstitious dread of Negroes, the members, taking advantage of the fact, visited insubordinate blacks and their white allies at dead of night to warn them to desist or decamp. The Pulaski example gave birth to imitators in other parts of Tennessee and in other Southern states, and in April 1867 a secret gathering at Nashville combined the units or "dens" under the name of the Invisible Empire of the South, with officers bearing awesome titles.

As time went on, violence became the chief reliance. Victims might now be beaten, maimed, or murdered. Criminal bands, too, adopted the eerie disguise for purposes of loot or private vengeance. In Louisiana alone, federal records show that 1,885 persons suffered injury or death during the 1868 presidential election year. The situation was already well out of hand when in January 1869 the "Grand Wizard" of the order decreed its dissolution. This action, however, only worsened conditions, for many of the dens refused to comply and the departure of the more responsible members gave the lawless elements full rein. Besides, scores of similar organizations had meanwhile sprung up, notably the Knights of the White Camelia, which, independently of the Klan, operated in the region from Texas to the Carolinas under the nominal control of a supreme council in New Orleans. The total number involved in these underground activities has been estimated at 550,000, though obviously the exact figure can never be known.

No other American extremist movement, before or since, has so brazenly defied the federal authority. Accordingly this has been the only instance (prior to the sporadic resistance to the school-desegregation decision of 1954 and the later civil rights acts) to bring down the might of the national government. In 1870 and 1871 Congress in successive laws empowered President Grant to end the societies with armed force if necessary and to appoint supervisors when required to assure Negroes full voting rights in federal elections. Soon hundreds of accused were arrested, United States troops reappeared in the South, and for a time the writ of habeas corpus was suspended in nine South Carolina counties. Consequently "Ku Kluxing" virtually ceased early in 1872. By then, however, the resourceful whites had learned they could frighten Negroes away from the polls by the mere threat of maltreatment. Later on, of course, when the South recovered full control of its affairs, they secured the same end by intricate election laws and the falsifying of returns.

The flare-up of intolerance to follow originated in the Midwest, being the handiwork of an anti-Catholic secret society, the American Protective Association. Founded in 1887 by one Henry F. Bowers, a lawyer of Clinton, Iowa, the APA reflected not only the ancient Protestant hostility to Catholicism but also, more directly, rural dislike of the rapidly growing cities, where the bulk of the Catholics resided, as well as urban resentment of the economic competition due to the mounting immigration from the papist countries of Southern and Eastern Europe. Every initiate swore to oppose "the diabolical work of the Roman Catholic Church" and, specifically, to hire or vote for none of its communicants or condone their appointment as teachers in the public schools.

As the membership spread east and west through the land, the principal features of the earlier Know-Nothing agitation were reproduced and expanded. "Escaped nuns" and "ex-priests" recited their shocking tales. Anti-Catholic weeklies and pamphlets whipped up passion. Forged documents, including an alleged encyclical commanding the faithful to "exterminate all heretics" on a given day in 1893, exposed Rome's designs against democratic Protestant America. A whispering campaign reported the collecting of arms in Catholic church basements. Mob violence likewise erupted, a Boston collision in 1895 causing the death of one man and the injury of many others. As a dismayed contemporary said of the APA, "In the name of freedom it stabs freedom in the dark; in the name of Christianity . . . it uses the weapons of the devil."

The members as a rule operated within the fold of the Republican party, since Irish Catholics comprised a mainstay of the Democrats. Assisted by self-styled patriotic societies with similar aims, the APA helped win many city and a number of state elections, contributed to William McKinley's victory in his race for governor of Ohio in 1893, and claimed one hundred supporters in Congress the following year. At its peak in late 1894 it probably numbered 100,000 persons, with the greatest concentration in the Middle West. By the 1896 presidential campaign, however, the bitter strife of the major parties over free silver and Bryanism obliterated the "Catholic menace" from the voters' minds, and the order disappeared from view.

The first outburst of zealotry in the present century was a throwback to both the Ku Klux Klan and the American Protective Association. Indeed, the new organization appropriated the name and methods of the Reconstruction body besides being itself Southern-born. Established in 1915 at Atlanta by William J. Simmons, an erstwhile itinerant preacher, it pledged its members to eliminate from political life all but white native-born Protestants. "By some scheme of Providence," Simmons declared, "the Negro was created a serf." Georgia already had a record of leading the Union in the number of its colored lynchings.

Because of the distracting effects of World War I, however, the resuscitated Klan made little headway until peace returned. Then alarm over the prospective deluging of the country by impoverished and perhaps revolutionary comers from devastated Europe caused it to extend rapidly through the South and Midwest, with strong outposts elsewhere as well; and in course of doing so it added animosity toward Jews to the older hatred of Negroes, Catholics, and immigrants. The anti-Semitism, long dormant but never before an overt issue, rested avowedly on a set of fraudulent documents of obscure Russian origin, *The Protocols of the Elders of Zion*. These allegedly unveiled a plot to assert Jewish predominance of the entire globe. As regards the United States, a contributor in the Klan organ, *The Searchlight*, offered to prove that Jews were already engaged in inciting the Afro-Americans to a race war. He indeed avowed he had "never met a disloyal American who failed to be either foreign-born or a Semitic." Men so thinking turned a deaf ear when the *Oklahoma Leader* rebuked this "new sort of Christianity that would flog Christ for being a Jew and a foreigner."

The night-riding Klansmen in ghostly attire, dotting the landscape as they went with fiery crosses, employed threats, beatings, arson, and murder against their victims, white and colored, and these unfortunates in due course came to include upholders even of such causes as the League of Nations, evolution, and birth control. In 1922 the organization entered politics, dominating for a time the states of Ohio, Indiana, Oklahoma, Arkansas, Texas, California, and Oregon with spokesmen in Congress. It wielded enough influence in the 1924 Democratic convention to deny the presidential nomination to Alfred E. Smith, the Catholic governor of New York. A year later 40,000 Klansmen paraded down Washington's Pennsylvania Avenue. At its zenith the membership supposedly embraced between four and five million.

As in past instances of the kind, however, popular revulsion to brute force and lawlessness set in, hastened by revelations of financial and other misdoings of the leaders. In Indiana the scandals sent a "Grand Dragon," a Congressman, the mayor of Indianapolis, and various lesser officials to prison. Even before this, legislation in New York, Michigan, Minnesota, Iowa, Texas, and some other states had banned masked brotherhoods. Further evidence of the decline appeared in the Democratic nomination of Al Smith in 1928 and the same year saw the United States Supreme Court, in a case appealed from New York, denounce the Klan for "conduct inimical to personal rights and welfare" in taking the law secretly into its hands.

Of greener memory is the scaremongering associated with the term McCarthyism. This affair, different from its predecessors, was largely the work of one man operating from an important position in the federal government under the protection of Congressional immunity. As in the other episodes particular circumstances facilitated his success. The public, only recently recovered from the shock of World War II, faced with dread new perils to peace from the postwar aggressions of the Soviet Union on neighboring states, its acquisition of the atom bomb, and disclosures of several instances of Communist infiltration of the United States government. On top of all these, America's springing to arms to save Korea from Communism brought the danger vividly home to every segment of the population.

Senator Joseph R. McCarthy of Wisconsin, hitherto an inconspicuous figure, seized the opportunity to exploit the anxieties apparently in a compulsive desire to win national prominence. Starting in 1950 he recklessly accused federal officials, high and low, of connivance with Russia. He charged that the State Department was knowingly harboring scores of card-carrying Communists. As chairman of a Senate committee he further assailed in public hearings persons of unblemished probity in the military and foreign services, wrecking their reputations and ruining their careers. When General Eisenhower ran for President in 1952, even that popular hero omitted from a speech a tribute to George C. Marshall out of deference to the Wisconsin Senator who had branded the army chief of staff in World War II and later Secretary of State as a party to a "conspiracy, the world-wide web of which had been spun in Moscow."

Through the nation at large as well as in Congress, McCarthy, in the troubled state of the popular mind, rallied an impassioned following regardless of party. Though many people privately denounced his methods, only the bravest dared speak out lest they, too, be pilloried for disloyalty. In due time, however, the public grew tired of the cries of

"Wolf! Wolf!" when not one of McCarthy's accusations produced a court conviction. Violations of the constitutional rights of citizens came to loom larger than unsupported allegations of treason. The United States Senate itself administered the final blow when in December 1954 it adopted a resolution condemning McCarthy by the overwhelming vote of sixty-seven to twenty-two.

What did this series of extremist movements have in common? Their basic kinship lay in the purpose to deny to fellow citizens sacrosanct constitutional safeguards, whether freedom of religion, speech, and association, due process of law, the right of suffrage, or other guarantees. It is easy therefore to regard the upsurges as un-American. But, had they really been so, they would not all have been indigenous in origin and gathered the strength they did. The truth is that they reveal an aspect of the national character we tend to forget: the presence of impulses and forces which, though usually latent, are never dead and spring into life when conditions prove favorable.

Moreover, those affected, however credulous they may seem in retrospect, were by and large well-meaning persons believing earnestly that they were fighting dragons that threatened catastrophe to themselves and the country. This gave many of them a dedicated sense of participating for the first time in decisions of vital public concern. As soon, however, as the cause demonstrated vote-getting promise, politicians cannily used it to advance their personal fortunes. Only two of the movements, however, generated national parties, and neither outlasted the single campaign. The rest bored from within one or the other, or both, of the established organizations.

THE CITIZEN

The goals they sought naturally varied according to the special circumstances, but these were always unmistakably set forth, since people are more easily aroused when offered cure-alls for their worries. Xenophobia and Negrophobia received the highest priority. Ironically enough, the initial provocation, Antimasonry, made so transitory an impress that the later insurgencies commonly themselves assumed the form of oath-bound orders.

Emotion was the mainspring of all of them. "Grand Wizard" Simmons of the second Ku Klux Klan undoubtedly spoke for the lot in saying, "The Klan does not believe that the fact that it is emotional and instinctive, rather than coldly intellectual, is a weakness. All action comes from emotion, rather than from ratiocination." With this conviction the leaders freely resorted to misrepresentation, distortion, and the Big Lie; and their overwrought followers responded by persecuting persons who offered opposition. Bodily harm and arson or, in the case of the McCarthy paroxysm, character assassination constituted their notion of serving the public good instead of the slow and (to them) highly suspect workings of the law.

These repressive movements occurred with a certain regularity, as though a people noted for hard common sense in day-to-day doings had to break loose from time to time when dealing with public matters. About twenty years separated the crests of the four waves in the last century, and thirty years in the two of the present one, thus suggesting that the intervals are growing longer. Despite these differences, however, the outcome was in every case the same, for each upon reaching its peak speedily declined, as if the public, surprised at itself, suddenly recovered its balance.

Only once did federal legislation enter in as a factor. The United States is an undoctrinaire country, jealous for the rights and liberties of the individual; and if the testimony of history counts for anything, no movement built on prejudice is ever likely to gain more than a temporary hold.

Against this background the extremism of the Goldwater candidacy should be viewed. Superficially it surpassed all its forerunners by capturing the national convention of one of the two great parties and dictating its nominees and platform. The dramatic victory, however, resulted from the failure of the moderate or progressive Republicans to unite their strength against a determined and well-organized minority. The tail wagged the dog. When Goldwater declared in his acceptance speech, "Extremism in the defense of liberty is no vice. Moderation in the pursuit of justice is no virtue," one of his unsuccessful rivals expressed the general sentiment of the party in sternly rejoining, "To extol extremism— whether 'in defense of liberty' or 'in pursuit of justice'—is dangerous, irresponsible, and frightening." The weeks that followed the convention saw massive Republican defections.

From the start, then, the new leaders lacked the broad base of party support from which they had expected to operate. Beyond this they confronted a difficulty which a knowledge of the earlier agitations could have helped them solve. They did not define with clarity the enemy they were fighting and thus denied their followers an effective recruiting cry. Goldwater, on the one hand, pleaded nostalgically for a return to simpler government and greater state autonomy and, on the other, demanded an aggressive foreign policy—two positions hard to reconcile. In addition, his appeal was confused by the vigorous backing of the John

Birch Society and of the White Citizens Councils and scattered reincarnations of the Ku Klux Klan in the South. These groups, the first McCarthyistic and the others racist, advocated measures which Goldwater himself neither explicitly avowed nor disclaimed.

Finally, the Goldwater endeavor proved ill-timed. If these upheavals partake of a roughly cyclical character, as the evidence suggests, even a more ably conceived campaign could not have got very far in 1964, since not twenty or thirty years but only ten had elapsed since the previous eruption. As it was, Goldwater went down to disastrous defeat, winning only his home state of Arizona and five others in the South. Although these latter had usually been Democratic politically, they saw in his issue of states' rights a means of suppressing the Negroes' human rights. A polling organization, moreover, reported that three out of every four of the relatively few Republican votes he received nationally stemmed from party loyalty, not confidence in the man or his program.

The uniform failure of this procession of extremist movements, even when well managed, to make more than a fleeting impression in the past augurs that they will not fare better in the future. Efforts to intimidate or manhandle fellow Americans because of their personal or social views, or to achieve the same end through repressive legislation, can never hope to win the lasting favor of a people dedicated historically to the principles of fair play and the equal protection of the law.

Index

Index

Abolitionist movement, 104–111, 173
Acton, Lord, 20
Adams, George Burton, 35
Adams, Henry, 47, 60
Adams, John, 76, 78, 85, 96, 190; and Boston Massacre, 81, 84n; and mob violence, 91–92, 93; and Declaration of Independence, 97, 127–128
Adams, Samuel, 7, 79
Allies, 166
Alton, Ill., 130
American Colonization Society, 109
American Council of Learned Societies, 67
American Historical Association, 34, 57, 63–64
American Historical Review, 62
American Protective Association, 148, 186, 187
Americans, characteristics of, 4, 7, 11–16, 28, 29, 106, 130, 134–135, 138, 140, 142, 146, 150, 151–152, 154
Andrews, Charles M., 62, 63
Anthropology, 30
Anti-Semitism, 188
Antislavery, *see* Abolitionist movement
Archaeology, 20, 30
Archives, use of, 21, 25. *See also* Research; Scholarship
Aristocracy, Southern, 119–123
Arizona, 194
Armed Neutrality League, 160
Atkinson, Edward, 107
Atlanta, Ga., 188
Atlantic Charter, 167–168
Atlantic Ocean, 159, 160, 161
Austerfield, 55

Bacon's Rebellion, 55
Baltimore, Md., 123
Bancroft, George, 23, 34, 47
Barnes, Harry Elmer, 26
Batavia, N.Y., 180
Baur, F. C., 39
Beard, Charles A., 10, 64
Beecher, Henry Ward, 105
Bell, Alexander Graham, 131
Benison, Dr. Saul, 4, 6–7
Béranger, Pierre Jean de, 50
Bernard, Francis, 86
Borah, Senator William, 164
Boston, Mass., 105, 187; disorders in, 78, 79, 80, 81, 88; and slavery, 130
Boston Massacre, 76, 77, 81, 84, 89, 92
Boston Tea Party, 76, 79, 83, 89, 91, 92
Bowers, Henry F., 186

Index

Brace, Charles Loring, 99, 105, 108–109
Braintree, Mass., 91
Britain: riots against, 82, 86, 87, 88, 89; controversy with, 83, 90–93, 160; and slavery, 100; rivalry with France, 159, 160; Tories compensated by, 170; U.S. support for, 177–178. *See also* Intolerable Acts; Stamp Act; War of *1812*
Brooklyn, N.Y., 51
Brown, John, 78–79
Brush, C. F., 131
Butler, Samuel, 133

Calhoun, John C., 99
California, 100
Carpenters' Hall, Philadelphia, 127
Catholicism, 86, 147; fear of, 130, 182, 186–187, 188
Census: *1850*, 119–120, 123; *1870*, 43
Centennial Exposition, 131, 132
Century Magazine, 55, 56, 60
Charleston, S.C., 123
Charlestown, Mass., 182
Cheyney, Edward P., 36, 38
Chicago Evening Journal, 50
Churchill, Winston, 167
Cincinnati, Ohio, 130
Civil War, 30, 71, 162, 163, 173–175. *See also* Abolitionist movement; Slavery
Clay, Henry, 181
Climate, effects of, 116–117
Collective security, 157, 158, 166–168
Colleges: revolution in, 3–4; curriculum of, 10, 12, 141–142, 145; enrollments in, 140; standardization in, 142, 146; military training in, 142–143; faculties of, 143, 144–145; two-year, 144

Colonies: history of, 56, 59; life and ideas in, 60, 61; authorities on, 62; law enforcement in, 82. *See also* Britain; Mob violence; Public opinion
Columbia College, 57
Columbia University, 10, 24
Common man, importance of, 8–9, 11, 28, 63
Communists, 148, 190
Comparative history, 12
Compromise of *1850*, 101, 163
Congress, 148, 184, 186; military decisions of, 167, 172, 178–179; members of, 183, 187, 189
Connecticut, 170
Conservatism, 4, 13–14
Constitution, 171
Constitutional history, 25
Coolidge, Calvin, 146
Copperheads, 173–175
Cotton industry, 68, 71, 107
Cotton Supply Association, 107
Craig, Mary Jane, 48
Cuba, 109
Cultural history, 10–11, 14, 30, 43, 57, 64
Culture, mechanization of, 3, 154–155
Cyclical theory, 13–14, 35, 37

De Bow, J. D. B., 119, 125
Declaration of Independence, 94, 95, 127, 147, 152
Declaration of Rights, 96
Delaware, 183
Democracy: role of in history, 7; principles of, 128–129; in education, 144
Democratic party, 42, 175, 181, 184, 187, 189, 194
Detroit, Mich., 182
Dickinson, John, 76, 90

Index

Documents, use of, 39–40. *See also* Archives; Research; Scholarship

Douai, Dr. Adolf, 105

East India Company, 79, 82, 89

Economic history, 30

Education: history of, 10–11, 13, 43; laws concerning, 138, 139; potential of, 140–146; support for, 152. *See also* Colleges

Eggleston, Edward, 9–10, 26, 30; *The Beginners of a Nation*, 58, 59; *The Circuit Rider*, 51; *The End of the World*, 51; *A History of Life in the United States*, 51, 58, 59; *The Hoosier Schoolmaster*, 47, 50; *Little Corporal*, 50; *The Mystery of Metropolisville*, 51, 53; "The New History," 63–64; *The Transit of Civilization*, 59, 60, 61

Eighty Years Progress of the United States, 65

Eisenhower, Dwight D., 190

Elections, presidential, 13n, 181, 183, 187, 189, 190, 193–194

Emancipation Proclamation, 111

Emerson, Ralph Waldo, 15–16, 150

Ethnology, 30

Evolution, teaching of, 139

Falmouth, Me., 86

Family, role of, 12–13

Farragut, David G., 73, 175

Federal government, 31, 75, 106, 152–153

Federalists, 42, 170, 171

Field, David Dudley, 105

Fillmore, Millard, 183

First Continental Congress, 91

Fiske, John, 55, 163

Florida, 139

Fort Sumter, 173

Fox, Dixon Ryan, 11, 43

France, 159, 160, 162

Franklin, Benjamin, 68, 82n

Freedom of the Press, Commission on, 15

Frontier, passing of, 151, 153

Gage, General Thomas, 77–78, 82, 90

Gallup poll, 177–178

Garrison, William Lloyd, 173

Gaspee, 78, 84n, 88

Georgia, 121, 188

German-Americans, 182

Germany, war with, 160, 163–164, 165, 166–167, 177, 178

Gladstone, T. H., 106

Golden Hill, battle of, 80, 89

Goldwater, Barry, 193–194

Goodyear, Charles, 72

Grant, Ulysses S., 186

Greeley, Horace, 105, 184

Green, John Richard, 63

Greenslet, Ferris, 55, 63

Guadalupe Hidalgo, treaty of, 172

Hale, Edward Everett, 106

Hamilton, Alexander, 73

Hancock, John, 80

Hansen, Marcus Lee, 12

Harding, Warren G., 165

Hartford Convention, 171

Harvard University, 10, 15, 24, 54, 56

Haskins, Charles H., 29

Hearth and Home, 50

Higher education, *see* Colleges

Historical writing: criteria for, 5, 6, 27; history of, 19–21; materials for, 20; influences on, 22–23; methodology in, 39; frailties in, 40–41, 42; statistical method in,

Index

42–43; novels as, 51, 53; and science, 68. *See also* Research

History: influence of economic factors on, 8, 10, 12, 27, 28, 29; uses of, 21; military, 25; modern school of, 26–27; definition of, 31, '35, 36–37, 38; evolution of, 33–34; limitations of research in, 34–35; generalizations of, 35–37; need for understanding of, 158

History of American Life, 64

History of the People of the United States, 30

Hitchcock, G. M., 164

Hoover, Herbert, 165

House Committee on Un-American Activities, 148

Hughes, Charles Evans, 165

Hutchinson, Lt.-Gov. Thomas, 78, 80, 82, 87–88

Illinois, 174

Immigrants, 12, 149–150, 182

Independent, 50

Indiana, 138, 174, 189

Indians: support for, 12, 15; Eggleston study of, 50, 51, 56

Industries, 123–124, 153. *See also* Inventions

Intellectual history, 8, 10, 12

Internationalism, 4, 28–29. *See also* Peace

Intolerable Acts, 76, 83, 89

Intolerance, 130, 138–139, 154. *See also* Catholicism

Inventions, 13, 68–72, 132, 133, 151

Iowa, 117, 118n, 189; University of, 10

Irish-Americans, 176, 177, 182, 187

Isolationism, 4, 158, 159, 168, 176, 177

Italy, 165

Jackson, Andrew, 7, 23, 129, 162, 171, 181

Jamestown, Va., 56

Japan, 165

Jefferson, Thomas, 7, 77, 96, 97, 109; quoted, 16, 146; and Declaration of Independence, 94, 128, 147, 157

John Birch Society, 194

Johns Hopkins University, 24

Journal of Negro History, 12

Journalism, 10, 13, 43

Julian, George W., 184

Juries, 88

Kansas, 105, 106

Kansas-Nebraska Act, 105, 183

Kennedy, John F., 13, 15

Know-Nothing party, 183–184, 187

Kraus, Michael, 63

Ku Klux Klan, 138, 148, 184–185, 187–189, 192

Labor, free, 106, 150

Ladies' Repository, 50

Lake George, 55

Law, history of, 13

League of Nations, 158, 159, 163–164, 165

Lecky, W. E. H., 83–84

Legislators, intolerance of, 138–139

Lend-lease, 166, 168, 178

Lexington, Ky., 123

Liberalism, 13–14

Liberty, 80

Life expectancy, 71, 73–74

Lincoln, Abraham, 163, 172, 173, 174, 175

Literary Digest, 164, 177

Locke, John, 96n

Lodge, Henry Cabot, 158–159, 164, 165

Index

London, 82. *See also* Britain
Louisiana, 121, 185
Louisville, Ky., 123, 182
Lowell, James Russell, 150, 172

Macaulay, T. B., 6, 7, 63
Marshall, George C., 190
Maryland, 87, 120–121, 172, 183
Mason, George, 96
Masons, Order of, 180–182, 192
Massachusetts, 87–88, 89–90, 91, 170–171. *See also* Boston
Massachusetts United Labor Commission, 15
Mather, Cotton, 62
McCarthy, Joseph R., 15, 189–191, 192
McClellan, George B., 175
McKean, Thomas, 170
McKinley, William, 187
McMaster, John Bach, 30, 47, 60, 61
Mechanization, era of, 132–135, 137
Mexico, 163, 171–172
Michelet, Jules, 63
Michigan, 189
Milton, Ky., 49
Minnesota, 49, 189
Minorities, 12
Mississippi, 121
Mob violence: use of, 77–78, 105, 129–130, 170, 182, 185, 187; punishment of, 90–92; legislation against, 189
Mobile, Ala., 123
Monk, Maria, 182
Morgan, William, 180
Morison, Samuel Eliot, 15
Morris, Gouverneur, 91
Morse, Samuel F. B., 182
Motley, John Lothrop, 23, 34

Nashville, Tenn., 120, 122, 123, 185
National Association of Manufacturers, 148
Nationalism, 7, 28, 29
Naval operations, 159. *See also* Atlantic Ocean; Wars
Negroes: franchise for, 111; protection for, 186; Masons' fear of, 192. *See also* Slavery
Netherlands, 160
New England Emigrant Aid Company, 106
New Orleans, La., 116, 123, 162, 171, 185
New York, 87, 118n, 170, 189
New York City, 80, 88, 173, 182
New York Times, 105
New York Tribune, 173
Newport, R.I., 86
Niebuhr, B. G., 39
Niles, David K., 13
Norfolk, Va., 123
North, the: and slavery, 100, 102, 103–115 passim, 124; social and economic conditions in, 120, 123; contrasts with the South, 122; pro-Southern sentiment in, 173–174
North Carolina, 122n, 139
"Novanglus," *see* John Adams

Ohio, 173, 174; State University of, 10, 140
Olmsted, Frederick Law: *Cotton Kingdom*, 98, 110, 120–121; *A Journey in the Back Country*, 98, 109, 113; *A Journey in the Seaboard Slave States*, 98, 113; *A Journey through Texas*, 98, 103–104, 106; "Letter to a Southern Friend," 103–104, 106, 117–118
Oregon, 100, 139
Organizations, voluntary, 3, 13, 43,

Index

134–138, 153, 174, 183–184. *See also* Ku Klux Klan; Masons
Osgood, Herbert L., 59, 62
Otis, James, 76, 90, 95
Outlook, The, 52, 56

Pacific Ocean, 161
Paine, Thomas, 159
Palmer, Brig. Gen. John M., 162
Paltsits, Victor H., 8
Parker, Theodore, 106
Parkman, Francis, 23, 34, 47, 53
Parliament, *see* Britain
Peace: organization for, 157, 158, 166–168; failure to plan for, 162–165; sentiment for, 170–171
Pennsylvania, 56, 170, 181, 183
Philadelphia, Pa., 131, 132, 182
Philology, 39
Pilgrims, 54, 55
Political parties, 147–148, 159. *See also* Democrats; Federalists; Republicans; Whigs
Political science, 25, 29–30, 31, 39, 138
Political Science Quarterly, 62
Polk, James K., 171–172
Prescott, W. H., 23
Progressive movement, 10
Propaganda, 21
Protestantism, 186–187, 188
Protocols of the Elders of Zion, The, 188
Psychology, 44–45
Public opinion, 130–131, 137, 146, 170–171. *See also* Mob violence
Pulaski, Tenn., 184, 185
Puritanism, 40

"Quarantine," 166, 177
Quincy, Josiah, Jr., 81, 95–96

Radcliffe College, 11–12
Railroads, 69, 70, 71, 72
Ranke, Leopold von, 39
Reconstruction, 30, 163, 184, 188
Religion, 7, 10–11, 39, 40, 138
Republican party, 42, 106, 165, 175, 181, 183, 187, 193
Research, historical: nature of, 20–21; influences on, 21–22; methods of, 24–25; equipment for, 31. *See also* Archives; Documents; Eggleston; History; Scholarship
Revolution, American: historical view of, 20, 30; causes of, 90–93; Sons and Daughters of, 139; opposition to, 170. *See also* Britain; Colonies
Rhode Island, 172, 181
Rhodes, James Ford, 47
Richmond, Va., 123
Riots: causes and nature of, 79–81, 83, 84, 85–86, 182; indemnification for, 87–88, 89; punishment of, 88, 89. *See also* Mob violence
Robinson, James Harvey, 10, 26
Roosevelt, Franklin Delano, 13, 15, 149; and World War II, 160, 167–168, 178–179; demands for "quarantine," 166, 177
Roosevelt, Theodore, 34
Root, Elihu, 165

Sacco and Vanzetti, 15
St. Louis, Mo., 123
San Antonio, Texas, 104, 105
Saratoga, N.Y., 57, 160
Savannah, Ga., 123
Schlesinger, Arthur M.: *The Birth of the Nation*, 8, 14; *History of American Life*, 11, 12, 64; *In Retrospect*, 5, 13, 14; *New Viewpoints*, 1, 10, 12, 13; *Paths to the Present*, 1, 13; *The Rise of the*

Index

City, 11; "The Tides of National Politics," 13

Scholarship, 5, 15, 24, 31. *See also* Research

Schouler, James, 47

Science: historical view of, 10–11, 12, 13, 23–24, 41, 66–68, 75; history as, 38; effects of, on society, 132–135, 137

Scrooby, 55

Searchlight, The, 188

Secession, 109–110, 171, 173

Seelye, Mrs. Elwin, 51

Seward, William H., 181

Shotwell, James T., 10

Simmons, William J., 188, 192

Slavery: historical view of, 29; Eggleston's view of, 49; Olmsted's view of, 98–125; solutions to problem of, 108–109, 155, 163, 183–184; economic effects of, 118–119; social effects of, 124–125; Whig view of, 172. *See also* Abolitionist movement

Smith, Alfred E., 189

Social conditions: among slaves, 117–118; in the South, 124–125; of immigrants, 150; reform of, 154

Social history: historical views of, 8, 10, 12, 29–30, 32, 36–37, 38, 40, 60–61; science and, 68–69. *See also* Eggleston

Society: impact of, on science, 70–71; standardization of, 138, 142, 146

South: conditions in, 115, 118. *See also* Aristocracy; Olmsted; Slavery

South Carolina, 121, 122, 186

Soviet Union, 167. *See also* Communists

Spain, 160

Sparks, Jared, 22

Specialization, 35

Stamp Act, 87, 91

Standardization, 134–135, 138, 142, 146. *See also* Organizations

Stephens, Alexander H., 172

Stephenson, George, 70

Stevens, John, 70

Stevens, Thaddeus, 181

Stevenson, Adlai, 15

Students: training of, in history, 33, 67; and educational policy, 144

Suffrage, 111–112, 129, 152, 184, 186

Sumner, Charles, 173

Sunday School Teacher, 50

Taxation: protests against, 92. *See also* Boston Tea Party; Intolerable Acts; Mob violence; Stamp Act

Technology, *see* Science

Tennessee, 121, 139, 185

Terrell, William, 49

Texas, 105, 106, 107, 120, 189; and slavery, 100, 104, 106, 121, 125; social conditions in, 116, 117–118

Thierry, Augustin, 52–53, 63

Tocqueville, Alexis de, 115, 130

Tooker, L. Frank, 55

Tories, 170

Totalitarianism, 177

Townshend Revenue Act, 76

Trumbull, John, 86

Tübingen, University of, 39

Turner, Frederick J., 42

Tyler, Moses Coit, 53

Uncle Tom's Cabin, 125

United Nations, 157, 167

Vallandigham, Clement L., 174–175

Van Doren, Carl, 63

Index

Vermont, 172, 181
Virginia, 55, 116, 118, 170

War of *1812*, 160, 162, 170–171, 175
Wars: stimulus to science, 69; U.S. involvement in, 159, 160, 161, 170–179; military unpreparedness for, 161–162
Washington, George, 22, 73, 158
Washington, D.C., 162, 171
Weed, Thurlow, 181
Welfare state, 152
Wendell, Barrett, 62
"Wheelberghs," 178
Whig party, 42, 183; and uprisings, 77–79; 84; propaganda of, 81, 172; influence of, 89; Olmsted adherence to, 100, 101

White Citizens Councils, 194
Whittier, John Greenleaf, 106
Wilmot Proviso, 100
Wilson, James, 96
Wilson, Woodrow: and League of Nations, 159, 163–165; and World War I, 15, 176–177
Winsor, Justin, 54, 56
Wirt, William, 181
Wisconsin, 139
Wolf, F. A., 39
Women: role of, 11–12, 13; pioneer efforts for rights of, 130
Wood, Fernando, 173
World history, 30

Yale Review, 13